FRANCE with FRENCH PHRASES

Annabel Warrender, Michael Cotsell
and Sophie Brudenell-Bruce

Illustrated by Joseph McEwan

Designed by Graham Round
Edited by Jenny Tyler and Angela Wilkes

D0543049

The material in this book is also published as two
separate Usborne books with the titles:
Junior Guide to France and *Junior Guide to French*.

Part 1. Guide to France

Contents of Part 1

The name Usborne and the device are Trade Marks of Usborne Publishing Ltd.

First published in 1979 by
Usborne Publishing Ltd,
20 Garrick Street, London WC2E 9BJ,
England.
Printed in Belgium by Henri Proost & Cie,
Turnhout

How to Use this Book

This is a picture guide book packed with information about France. Take it on holiday with you and find out about lots of exciting things to see and do, or read it at home and find out what it is like in France.

It is a good idea to check with a local tourist office for opening times, admission fees and directions. Some places are closed during the winter and many are closed at least one day a week.

This book explains some of the new and strange sights, tells you what to eat and where to go, and suggests some fun things to do, such as going to puppet shows, watching people make wine or going ice-skating. It makes visits to châteaux and churches fun by telling you about things to spot in them. You can also find out about French shops and money.

Before you start your trip, collect as much information as you can about the area you are going to visit. There is a list of useful addresses and books on page 61. Don't forget to take your camera, a notebook for recording interesting things you see and do and coloured pencils for playing the numberplate game on page 60. Try to learn the French words for things you are specially interested in, so you will be able to ask about them when you get there.

There are lots of interesting things to spot. When you see something, put a tick in the little square next to the picture. You might be able to spot some things without even going to France, so keep your eyes open.

It is a good idea to save bus, Métro and entrance tickets, paper bags, sweet wrappers and anything else you can find so you can make a collection to remind you of your holiday. You probably won't be able to afford to save many coins, but you can make rubbings of them by putting them under a piece of paper and rubbing with a soft pencil or wax crayon, like this.

The map on page 5 shows many of the places mentioned in this book. For smaller places, the name of the *département* is given in brackets next to the name. You will find all the *départements* on the map on page 60.

Facts about France

The official name for France is La République Française. It is the largest country in Europe covering 551,500 sq.km. It is hexagonal in shape and joins on to six other countries.

Divisions of France

France was divided into *départements* in 1790. Each has a number and most are named after the main river running through them. There are 95 *départements* in mainland France. Each has a main town and a *Préfet* chosen by the President.

Government

The President appoints a Prime Minister and other ministers. They are responsible to Parliament, which consists of two houses, the National Assembly and the Senate. The National Assembly is elected by the people for 5 years. The Senate is elected for 9 years by local councillors.

Language

French is derived from Latin spoken by Roman Legionaries. The Breton language is still sometimes used in Brittany and the Basque language in the Pyrenees.

Main products

France is the largest agricultural nation in Europe. Its main crops are: sugar beet, wheat, potatoes and barley. France and Italy share the title of world's top wine producer and France is also the second world producer of cheese, and the leading producer of perfume. Main exports are motor vehicles especially Renault, Citroen and Peugeot. More than one car in ten of total world output is French.

The President

France's last king (Louis-Philippe) abdicated in 1848. The Head of State is now the President, who is elected every seven years by the French people. Since 1981 the President has been François Mitterrand.

The flag

This has been the French flag since the French Revolution in 1789. It is called the Tricolore and is made up of the red and blue colours of Paris and the white of the Bourbon kings.

Facts and figures

Population of France: 53,838,000
Five largest cities:
Paris   Lille
Lyon   Bordeaux
Marseille
Longest river: River Loire, 1,012km
Highest mountain: Mont Blanc, 4,807m

Public holidays

1 January: *le jour de l'an*
*Easter Monday: *le lundi de Pâques*
1 May: *le premier mai*
*Ascension Day: *l'Ascension*
*Whit Monday: *le lundi de la
Pentecôte*
14 July: *le 14 juillet*

15 August: *la fête de l'Assomption*
1 November: *la fête de la Toussaint
(All Saint's Day)*
11 November: *le 11 novembre
(Armistice Day)*
25 December: *Noël*
Dates change each year.

5

Money

French money, the franc, is made up of 100 centimes. You can find out how much the franc is worth in pounds or dollars at any bank.

On the **100 franc note** there is a picture of Corneille, a dramatist.

The **50 franc note** shows the head of Jean Racine, a 17th century French dramatist.

The **10 franc note** has recently been changed and made smaller. The new one shows Berlioz, the composer.

Here are the French coins. Learn to recognize them so you do not make mistakes in shops.

10 centimes

5 centimes

5 francs (1 franc and ½ franc coins are similar, but smaller.)

10 francs

20 centimes

6

Shopping and Eating

When you are abroad, it is fun to go round the shops and see the different kinds of things they sell. Here you can see some of the most useful places to shop. On the next page you can find out what all the smaller shops sell.

Outside most large towns there are enormous, new **shopping centres** with their own car parks. You can buy anything you want there, from food to furniture, and everything is cheaper than it is in smaller shops.

Most towns have a **market** once or twice a week in the main square. You can buy fresh food there and may even see live rabbits and chickens for sale.

MONOPRIX □

prisunic 🎗
□

The **department stores** in France are fun to look around. Other good places to shop are the cheap chain stores, such as *Monoprix* and *Prisunic*. Look for these signs.

Where to eat

Cafés are a very important part of French life. You can go there to drink or meet your friends. They are open from early in the morning until late at night.

A café called a **brasserie** sells draught beer. The word "brasserie" means brewery. You can often get simple meals and snacks in them too.

France has some of the most famous, expensive **restaurants** in the world, such as Maxim's in Paris. But there are many good, inexpensive restaurants.

Look out for signs like this along main roads. **Les Routiers** (lorry drivers') restaurants are open to everyone and serve good food at reasonable prices.

The Shops

Maison de la Presse. You can buy comics, newspapers, maps and paperbacks here.

Papeterie. This is a stationer's shop. It sells writing paper and everything children need for school.

Librairie. This is a book shop, not a library.

Tabac. Tobacconist's where you can also buy stamps and sweets. Look for the red sign.

Confiserie. This is a rather expensive kind of sweet shop.

Pâtisserie. You can buy pastries and cakes here. Sometimes there is a tea-room as well.

Boulangerie. You can buy fresh bread here. The bakery is often at the back of the shop.

You can buy chips and drinks from the **frites (chips) van.**

Vans and stalls sell **crêpes**, pancakes with lots of different fillings.

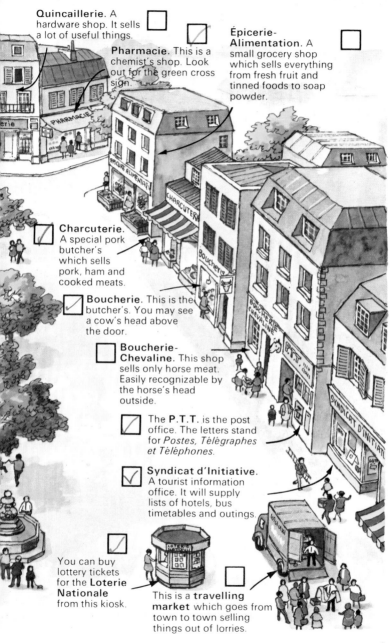

Quincaillerie. A hardware shop. It sells a lot of useful things.

Pharmacie. This is a chemist's shop. Look out for the green cross sign.

Épicerie-Alimentation. A small grocery shop which sells everything from fresh fruit and tinned foods to soap powder.

Charcuterie. A special pork butcher's which sells pork, ham and cooked meats.

Boucherie. This is the butcher's. You may see a cow's head above the door.

Boucherie-Chevaline. This shop sells only horse meat. Easily recognizable by the horse's head outside.

The **P.T.T.** is the post office. The letters stand for *Postes, Télégraphes et Téléphones*.

Syndicat d'Initiative. A tourist information office. It will supply lists of hotels, bus timetables and outings.

You can buy lottery tickets for the **Loterie Nationale** from this kiosk.

This is a **travelling market** which goes from town to town selling things out of lorries.

9

French Food

France is famous for its food and drink. The French have always taken food seriously and are very good cooks. Try to eat as many different things as you can. Here are some dishes to look out for and try.

Most of the **oysters** eaten in Europe come from Brittany. They are served in their shells and eaten raw.

Mussels (*moules*) are sometimes eaten raw. But they are often cooked and served in a white wine sauce.

Snails (*escargots*) are a great delicacy. They are served in their shells and eaten with a special fork.

Frogs' legs taste a bit like chicken. They are usually lightly fried and you eat them with your fingers.

Homard à l'armoricaine is a lobster dish from Brittany. The lobster is served in a spicy tomato sauce.

Boeuf bourguignon is a famous stew from Burgundy. It is made from beef cooked in red Burgundy wine.

Cassoulet comes from the south-west of France. It is a stew made from white beans and goose, duck or sausage meat.

Bouillabaisse is a speciality of Provence. It is a fish soup which may contain over 20 different kinds of fish.

Quiche lorraine comes from Lorraine. It is a delicious open tart filled with eggs, cream and bacon.

Salade niçoise is a speciality of Nice. It is a salad of olives, anchovies, tomatoes, onions and tuna fish.

Pâté de foie gras is a rich pâté made from goose liver and often stuffed with a rare fungus called truffles.

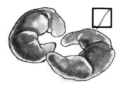 

A **baguette** is the famous long French loaf with a crisp crust. You must eat it soon after it is baked.

Croissants are flaky, crescent-shaped rolls. People eat them for breakfast and often dip them into their coffee.

Brioches are a kind of sweet, soft bread bun, usually shaped like a small cottage loaf.

 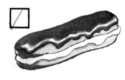 

A **petit pain au chocolat** is a small flaky pastry roll with chocolate in the middle. Children eat them for tea.

Éclair. One of the most famous French pastries. Usually filled with a specially flavoured cream.

Crêpes. These pancakes are a speciality of Brittany. They can have sweet or savoury fillings.

Herbs and flavourings

 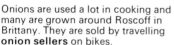 

Onions are used a lot in cooking and many are grown around Roscoff in Brittany. They are sold by travelling **onion sellers** on bikes.

Bay leaves and garlic are used to add flavour to dishes. You will often see **bay trees** outside restaurants.

A French meal

French people eat their main meal at midday, when they have a two-hour lunch-break. They usually start the meal with soup or crudités (raw salad vegetables). Next they have a meat or fish course. They often eat their vegetables or green salad after this. They finish the meal with cheese, then fruit or pudding.

Wine, Cheese and Newspapers

France is famous for making good wine. There are several wine growing areas and each one produces a different kind of wine. You can tell where a wine comes from by the shape of its bottle. Here are the main ones to spot.

Champagne

Burgundy

Bordeaux   Alsace   Côtes de Provence

Wine labels

You can find out a lot about the wine in a bottle from its label. Here are some of the things it tells you.

The year it was made (vintage).

The vineyard owner.

Bottled at the place where it was made.

CHATEAU BELAIR

SAINT EMILION
Appellation Saint Emilion
Contrôlée
1959
Edouard Dubois Challon
Proprietaire a Saint Emilion
MIS EN BOUTEILLES AU CHATEAU

The name of the estate.

The area the wine comes from.

Appellation Contrôlée means that the wine is good. Strict A.C. regulations control where wines come from and how they are made.

Other drinks

An apéritif is drunk before a meal to whet your appetite. **Pernod** tastes of aniseed and is very popular.

Cognac and **Kirsch** are drunk after meals. Cognac is brandy and Kirsch is a liqueur made from cherries.

Chartreuse is a green liqueur made from herbs and honey. Monks used to make it and still control how it is made.

French beer usually tastes like lager. Most of it is made in Alsace, where a lot of hops are grown.

Cider is made in Normandy and Brittany, where there are many orchards. You can buy it at supermarkets.

The main French bottled mineral waters are **Évian**, which is still, and **Perrier**, which is fizzy.

Newspapers and magazines

It is fun to look at all the different newspapers, magazines and comics when you are in France. Here are the main ones to look out for.

Le Monde and **Le Figaro** are the two main national daily papers. People either receive them by post or buy them at news stands or shops as there are no paper boys.

You will see a lot of weekly news magazines, such as **Paris Match,** and women's magazines, such as **Elle. Pif** is one of a big range of weekly comics.

Cheese

France makes over 350 different kinds of cheese, and every area has its specialities. Cheese goes well with wine and the French often finish a meal with cheese and fruit, rather than with pudding. Here are some cheeses for you to try.

Brie and **Camembert** are round cheeses with a soft, creamy centre and a smooth white powdery crust.

Roquefort is a strong blue-veined cheese made from ewes' milk and left to mature in caves in Languedoc.

Fromage au Marc de Raisin is a round, sweet cream cheese rolled in a crust of grape seeds.

Chèvre is strongly flavoured goats' milk cheese. It is sometimes wrapped in straw and vine leaves.

Petit Suisse is a creamy, non-salted cheese, rather like smooth cottage cheese.

What to See and Do in Paris 1

Here are some things to spot on the streets of Paris, the capital of France and the fifth largest city in the world. Paris grew up along the banks of the River Seine over 2,000 years ago, and has been a centre for scholars and artists since the Middle Ages. Clues to the city's long history can be seen in the old churches, monuments and palaces lining the busy streets.

Some old Métro stations have **decorated ironwork entrances** in the *Art Nouveau* style, popular in the early 1900s.

Shops and businesses often had **picture signs** to show what they sold or made. You can still see some.

Wrought-iron was often used for decoration. Look out for **double-sided benches** like this one.

This is an **advertise-ment column**. Since 1881, it has been against the law to stick posters on the walls.

Wallace Fountain. One of a hundred drinking fountains given to Paris in the 1800s by an Englishman called Sir Richard Wallace.

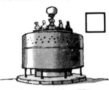

This is a **pissoir,** or street lavatory for men. They are a rare sight now, as they are being replaced by modern inside toilets.

Plaques on walls show where famous people once lived or important events took place.

There are many different kinds of **street lamps** in Paris. Some of the more elaborate ones date back to the time when gas street lighting was first introduced. See how many you can spot.

Street life

The **Bouquinistes** have open-air stalls on the banks of the Seine. They sell old books, maps and pictures.

There are many **street painters** in Montmartre. Famous artists like Renoir and Picasso once lived here.

On the Ile de la Cité there is a **flower market** every day except Sunday, when there is a bird market instead.

There is a **bird market** on the Quai de la Mégisserie. Birds used to be set free when the king came to Paris.

The Flea Market, at the Porte de Clignancourt, sells old clothes, antique furniture and junk.

On fine days you may see a **pavement artist** like this one. When it rains, his picture will be washed away.

Pavement cafés are a common Paris sight. Notice the waiters with white cloths over their arms.

You can sometimes see **mime** (silent) actors in the street. Notice the white make-up on their faces.

At **street bookstalls** you can buy newspapers, magazines, postcards, guide books and even lottery tickets.

The river

This is the **Pont Neuf** or "new bridge". In fact it is the oldest bridge in Paris.

Pont Alexandre III is covered with lamps and statues. It was built in 1900 for a world exhibition.

This **small Statue of Liberty** is on the Pont de Grenelle. The original in New York was built by Eiffel.

15

What to See and Do in Paris 2

You can get an amazing view of Paris from the steps of the **Sacré Coeur** church, on the hill of Montmartre.

The **Place de la Concorde** is where Louis XVI was guillotined during the Revolution in 1793.

The **Arc de Triomphe** was built to celebrate the victories of Napoleon. The Tomb of the Unknown Soldier is under it.

Notre-Dame was begun in AD1160 and took 200 years to build. The carvings on the doors tell Bible stories.

The **Eiffel Tower** was built in 1889 for a great exhibition. The 320m high tower was the world's tallest building for 40 years.

Thousands of people were imprisoned in the **Conciergerie** before going to the guillotine during the French Revolution. You can still see Marie-Antoinette's cell.

The 19th century **Opéra** is one of the largest theatres in the world. The stage can hold 450 performers.

One of the most famous night-clubs in Paris is the **Moulin Rouge** (Red Windmill). Look for the windmill on the roof.

In the 19th century, many wide, open streets or **boulevards** were built. One of the most famous is the Champs-Élysées.

Paris is still a centre for fashion. Look out for **shops of famous designers,** like Cardin, St Laurent and Dior.

Interesting museums

At the **Jeu de Paume** you can see colourful paintings like this one of ballet dancers by Degas. *Métro: Concorde*

The vast **Louvre** museum was once a royal palace. Try to find the armless statue of "Venus de Milo" and Leonardo da Vinci's painting of the "Mona Lisa". *Métro: Louvre or Palais-Royal*

The **Musée Grévin** has life-size wax models of famous people, such as Napoleon and Josephine, in scenes from French history. *Métro: Montmartre*

Weapons and uniforms, including Napoleon's overcoat, are on show at the **Musée de l'Armée.** *Métro: St-François-Xavier*

At the **Musée National des Arts et Traditions Populaires,** you can see objects from everyday life in old France; such as regional costumes, toys, musical instruments, fairground animals and games. *Métro: Sablons*

Go to the **Musée de la Monnaie** to see coins and medals, and, on some days, the workshops of the Mint. *Métro: Pont-Neuf*

The **Palais de la Découverte** is a planetarium and science museum. Look our for the moon rock. *Métro: Franklin-Roosevelt*

The **Musée National des Techniques** has early planes, robots, trains

and clockwork dolls. *Métro: Réaumur-Sébastopol*

What to See and Do in Paris 3

The Jardin d'Acclimation in the Bois de Boulogne has a small zoo, a dolphinarium, donkey rides, puppet shows, miniature cars and a miniature train that leaves from the Porte Maillot. *Métro: Sablons*

Puppet shows are held every afternoon in the Jardin du Luxembourg (off Boulevard St Michel) and the Parc de Choisy. *Métro: Place d'Italie*

You can go **rowing** on the lakes in the Buttes-Chaumont Park *(Métro: Botzaris)* and in the Bois de Boulogne and the Bois de Vincennes.

The biggest **zoo** in Paris is in the Bois de Vincennes *(Métro: Porte Dorée)* open from 9.00 a.m. to 5.30 p.m. Look out for the fake mountain near the bear pit.

You can go **skateboarding** at the Villette Skate Parc *(Métro: Porte de la Villette)* every day but Monday. They will let you hire all the necessary equipment there too.

The Cirque Gruss *(Métro: Rambuteau or Hôtel de Ville)* recreates **circus** acts from old paintings.

The Théâtre du Petit Monde, 252 Faubourg St-Honoré, shows. **plays** for children every Wednesday and Saturday.

The Studio Marigny, Carré Marigny cinema (tel. 225 20 74) shows **films** for children all through the year.

Exciting places to go

One of the best ways of seeing Paris is from the river in a **Bateau Mouche**. Boats leave from the Pont de l'Alma, Pont Neuf and Pont d'Iéna.

The **Georges-Pompidou Centre** sometimes has special children's exhibitions. You can have exciting rides on the long escalators which are enclosed in plastic tubes. *Métro: Rambuteau*

On most Saturdays, you can visit the **catacombs** and see millions of old skeletons. Take a torch. *Métro: Denfert-Rochereau.*

You can go on a guided tour of the **radio and television** studios at the Maison de la Radio. *Métro: Passy*

You can take a **boat trip along the sewers** under Paris on certain days.

Buses and Trains

The easiest way to get about Paris is by underground, the Métro. Trains run about every five minutes, from 5.30 a.m. to 1.15 a.m. There is also an express service (R.E.R.) to the suburbs. Buses run from 6.30 a.m. to 8.30 p.m., and some run until midnight.

This is a **Métro sign**. Look out for the old *Art Nouveau* ones. The 348 métro stations are about 500m apart.

Métro tickets are sold at all stations. There is only one fare. It is cheaper to buy a *"carnet"* of 10 tickets.

There is one **1st class carriage**, painted pale yellow, which stops next to this sign above the platform.

You can use your Métro tickets on **buses** too. Punch your ticket in the machine by the door when you get on the bus. Ring the bell when you want to get off and leave by the doors in the middle of the bus.

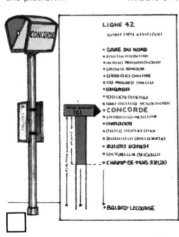

All **bus stops** are request stops. The red arrow on the timetable points to where you are on the route. If you are going further than the red section, you need two tickets. Check that you are going in the right direction.

French railways are called the S.N.C.F. You can buy tickets at a station or at a travel agent's. It is best to buy them in advance and to reserve a seat.

Before you go on to the platform, punch your ticket in one of these machines. An inspector will check and collect it when you are on the train.

On the Road 1

Main roads are called *Routes Nationales*. They all have numbers which are shown on red signposts. Minor roads have yellow signposts. You must always wear a seat belt in a car. Here are some things to look out for when you are travelling on French roads.

The Citroën Deux Chevaux (Two Horse-Power) and the **Renault 4** are the two most common types of car in France.

Police Car. Get out of its way as quickly as you can if it is sounding its siren.

Fire Engines. These go to all emergencies, including road accidents.

Ambulance. Most of these are privately owned, often by the local taxi service. They can be very expensive.

Mopeds. You will see lots of people riding these around French towns. You can ride one when you are 14.

Number Plates. The last two numbers show which *département* the car comes from. See page 60 for a number-plate game.

Lorries and caravans have special **speed limit numbers** on the back. The higher one is for motorway driving.

In France, you drive on the right-hand side of the road. This was started by Napoleon's regiment, the Garde Républicaine.

(a) (b) (c)

Road Signs. (a) This is a *borne kilométrique*. It shows the distance to nearby towns, and often your height above sea level. (b) Fire signs warn of the danger of fire in dry areas. (c) A yellow diamond shows you have the right of way.

This sign means you must not go faster than 50 k.p.h. Similar round blue signs mean you must not go slower than 50 k.p.h.

On the Road 2

Motorways
(autoroutes) are
numbered — e.g. A6.
You usually have to
pay a toll *(péage)* to
drive along them.

Many péages are
automatic. You throw
the right amount of
coins into the basket,
and the barrier rises.

Windsocks on windy
stretches of road are to
help drivers judge the
wind's force and
direction.

Many **roads in flat areas are lined with trees.**
These provide shade and act as a wind-break. The
most common tree are poplars.

Look out for unusual
water towers. They
are usually just outside
towns or villages.

Special tall **vineyard
tractors** are used in
the wine-growing areas
to weed between the
rows of grape vines.

Large areas of farmland have to be kept watered
during the summer when there is not much rain.
Look out for great shoots of water from large
automatic sprinklers.

You will often see
**wayside crosses and
shrines** at the side of
the road, especially on
old pilgrims' routes.

All towns and villages have a **sign showing the
name of the place** as you enter its boundaries.
When you leave the town, there is another name
sign with a line through it.

Villages

There are many different kinds of towns and villages in France. There is often a particular reason why they have been built where they are, such as the need for water or safety. Here are some of the special types of village you might come across.

In the south of France you will see many **hill-top villages**. They were built like this partly to be safe from attack and partly to keep the good soil in the valleys clear for farming.

Fortified towns, called *bastides*, were built during the Middle Ages, when there were many wars. This is Carcassonne, a bastide in South-West France.

The people who built *bastides* gave the same name to many of their towns. Look out for any **towns with these names.** They were all built in the 1200s.

Villages were sometimes built **round a castle or monastery,** which protected the peasants and gave them work. This is Mont-St-Michel in Brittany.

In mountainous regions some villages were built right **at the edge of a cliff,** so that the villagers could spot enemies approaching.

Spa towns, like Évian and Vichy, were built wherever there was a natural spring containing health-giving minerals. The water is often bottled, like this, and sold.

In the past twenty years, many **new towns** have been built, often as an extension to an existing town. Some have strange, modern buildings, like these at Crécy.

23

Towns

Many large modern towns and cities date back to the Middle Ages. If you follow the signs saying *Centre Ville* you will come to the old quarter. Here are some of the things you can look for there.

Wall fortifications, with towers, battlement walks and entrance gates. Often these are ruined.

The old part of the town often has narrow medieval streets, with **half-timbered houses.**

The **town hall** (*Hôtel de Ville*) flies the French flag. Some town halls in the north are very ornate.

Medieval belfry. The bells were rung to warn the citizens of fire or that enemies were approaching.

The **town clock** is often very ornate, a reminder of how important it once was when only rich people could afford a clock.

Old **market halls** are still used in market towns. They usually look like barns with stone pillars.

There is a **square** in the middle of most towns and villages. All the main shops are grouped around it.

Large town houses were often built around a **courtyard** after the 1600s. They were owned by noblemen.

You will see a lot of **wrought-iron balconies** in French towns. They were built at the beginning of the 1900s.

If you get the chance, look into some of the **tiny courtyards** inside buildings. Gardens are often hidden there.

A lot of French people live in flats. A caretaker (**concierge**) looks after all the flats in the block.

Most towns have a decorative **public garden,** with low hedges and a fountain.

In the main square of the town you will often see **statues** of famous people who once lived there.

Policemen in towns are called **agents de police** and wear blue uniforms. They will help you if you get lost.

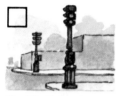

Traffic lights have small lights halfway down the post, so that you can see them more easily from a car.

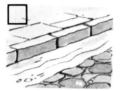

You will sometimes see **water being hosed along the streets** in the morning, to keep them clean.

The **town cemetery** is often just outside the town, away from the church, except in small villages.

At week-ends and on summer evenings, you will often see groups of men playing **boules.** This is a game rather like bowls. The men throw metal balls towards a small marker ball, and points are scored for the balls nearest to the marker. Boules is usually played in a park or square, where the ground is flat.

In small villages, you may still see groups of women doing their washing at a **communal laundry.**

Before houses had running water, the well or **water pump** was an important place in the village.

In the south-west, you may see people playing **pelota.** Men wearing gloves hit a ball against a wall.

Houses I

Old houses were built out of local materials, and vary in colour according to the type of soil or stone in the area. Here are some different types of houses to spot. Some are in the countryside, some in the towns, so keep your eyes open.

Cave House. In some places, such as the Dordogne a few people live in caves in the chalk hills.

Cob. Made from a mixture of mud paste and straw. One of the oldest kinds of building materials.

You will see **rough stone houses** all over France. Corners, windows and doorways are often outlined in brick or smooth stone.

Tile-hung houses have wooden or slate tiles covering the top storeys. Look out for houses like this in Picardy and northern France.

Whitewash, a mixture of lime and crushed earth or sand, often covers stone houses. Sometimes it is lightly coloured to soften the glare of the sun.

Brick houses are quite rare as it is cheaper to use stone. They are usually larger houses. Corners, doors and windows are usually edged with stone.

Smoothed and neatened stone slabs are used for grander houses in limestone regions, where the stone is softer and cuts easily. Doors and windows are often decorated.

Brick and **stone** are sometimes combined to make a pattern of different colours and shapes. You will see these in Normandy, Béarn and Languedoc.

Wooden houses

Patterned wooden houses like this can be found in Alsace. They usually have lots of balconies and window boxes.

Alpine chalet. The upper storey is made of wooden planks with no windows. Grain is stored up there.

Box-frame houses. The wooden frame is filled in with stone. The downstairs is usually all stone.

Diamond pattern houses have brick or stone filling the spaces in the wooden frame.

Look for this kind of **half-wooden house** in Normandy. Upright pillars of wood are used close together.

Farmhouses

Many French farmhouses have the farm buildings and living rooms under the same roof.

In the big farming areas such as the Languedoc, houses are long and low, with farm buildings attached to the house on either side.

Richer farmers in the north and west of France have their farms arranged around a courtyard. Look out for elaborate gate-posts.

This kind of stone farmhouse has the cellar and stables downstairs. An outside staircase leads to the living rooms.

Crops are stored in the granary in the tall loft of this farmhouse. A ladder or outside staircase leads to the roof.

Look for these little round houses in mountain regions. Farmers use them in summer.

27

Houses 2
Roofs

 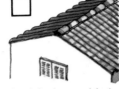 

Tall gabled roof, with two steeply sloping sides, so rain runs off easily. See these in the north and mountain regions.

Look for **low gabled roofs,** with gently sloping sides, in the south where there is less rain.

Hipped roofs have slopes on all sides.

Low gabled roofs with jutting out sides are used in snowy places. The snow stays on top and keeps the house warm.

Mansard roofs were originally designed to avoid a tax on windows in the walls.

Overhanging roofs with wooden supports shelter the front of the house. They often jut out over a porch or window.

Gable-ends are often decorative. Look out for these.

Corble-steps or Crow-steps.

Dutch gables have curly edges.

Curved gables look like a moustache.

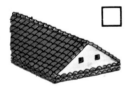  

Roman tiles, made from clay, are curved and interlocking. Look for them mainly in Provence.

Flat tiles. Either made from red clay or grey slate. You will usually see them on tall sloping roofs.

Scalloped tiles. Made from slate or wood. They are often on tile-hung houses and curved turret roofs.

Roof decorations

In eastern France, you may see **coloured glazed pottery tiles** made into a pattern like this.

Thatch is made from straw or reeds. In the past, most small farmhouses were covered in thatch.

Thatched roofs often have **flowers** growing along the top. People believed they stopped witches from landing.

Weathercocks. These sometimes indicate the house-owner's job. This is probably a sailor's house.

Look out for **pottery animals** sitting on house roofs.

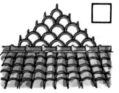

Pottery vases are sometimes put on the gable-ends.

This decoration is called an "épi". You will see different designs.

Bouquets de Baptême, are sometimes put up to celebrate the completion of the house.

Sarrasin chimneys, like these, are about 400 years old. You will see them in the Bourgogne area.

Storks sometimes **nest** on the chimney pots in Alsace.

29

Windows and Doorways

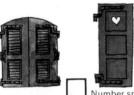

Number spotted

Nearly every house has **shutters** to protect and decorate the windows. They keep out bad weather and the glare of the sun. Here are three different types. See how many you can spot.

Nearly all windows **open inwards.** They are often tall, like doors. This is why glass doors are often called "French windows".

There are often little **balconies** outside, which are used to hang washing out and air the bedding.

Dormer windows, set into the tall sloping roofs, are often quite elaborate. They are sometimes the doors to the granary at the top of the house. Here are three different types to spot.

Look out for **dates, inscriptions** or **sculptures** above the doorways.

A Guardian Angel is often carved above stable doors in Brittany.

In Provence, you will often see a **tall cypress tree** on either side of the doorway. This is a very ancient custom, possibly dating back to Roman times, when it is thought they showed soldiers on the march where to find water.

Some grander houses may have a **coat-of-arms** above the door.

Country Buildings

Many people keep pigeons, which they eat. They are kept in buildings called **pigeonniers,** either near the house, or attached to it like a tower. At one time only the rich lords were allowed to own one, and some of the older ones are quite grand. Look for holes where the birds fly in and out.

Turret pigeon house

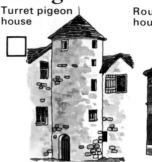

Round pigeon house

You will sometimes see little stone huts in the fields. These are called **bories.** They were used to keep sheep and goats in at night.

You will see lots of **goats** in France The farmers put bells round their necks so they can find them easily.

Mills

Watermills have a large wheel which is turned by the flow of a stream. Often the water runs into a millpond.

Very few **windmills** are still in working order. Look for stone or wood ones. Some have thatched roofs. The sails were built so they could be tipped sideways in bad weather to stop them being torn off by strong winds.

Wells

In the past people got their water from **wells.** In some places they are still used by people who do not have taps in their houses. Look for wells in farmyards and village squares. Some have dates carved on them. You will find many that were built about 100 years ago.

Wells are often built of stone with a wooden handle. Sometimes they have roofs to keep the water clean.

31

Prehistoric France

Stone Age people were living in France over 40,000 years ago, so there are some very old prehistoric remains to be seen.

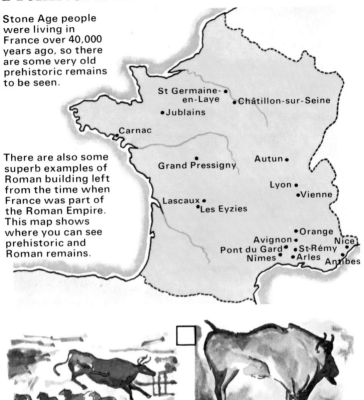

St Germaine-en-Laye • Châtillon-sur-Seine
• Jublains
Carnac
Grand Pressigny • Autun •
Lyon •
• Vienne
Lascaux • • Les Eyzies
• Orange
Avignon • Nice
Pont du Gard • • St-Rémy
Nîmes • • Arles Antibes

There are also some superb examples of Roman building left from the time when France was part of the Roman Empire. This map shows where you can see prehistoric and Roman remains.

There are many **cave paintings** in south-western France which are over 40,000 years old. The most famous, found at Lascaux by some children, are no longer open to the public. But there are several other painted caves in the Dordogne which you can visit.

Carvings. Only a few prehistoric tombs in Europe are carved and most of these are in Brittany.

Menhir. Single standing stone, over 4,000 years old. Some are over 6m tall.

Christianized menhir. Christian symbols, such as crosses, were later carved on some menhirs.

Dolmen. Two menhirs covered with a large slab, called a "table stone", which may be up to 6m wide. Probably once a tomb.

Alignment. Lots of menhirs arranged in parallel lines. The most famous are around Carnac, in Brittany. Experts think they may have been used for funeral processions, or by astrologers charting the planets.

Cromlech. Several menhirs grouped together in a circle. Like the alignments, they may have had a religious or astrological use.

Tumulus. Vast, ancient burial chamber, covered over with earth and grass. This one, at Cuniac in Brittany, is 20m high and 260m round.

Things to look for in museums

You can see some very ancient prehistoric objects in French museums. Here are some to look out for. Look out also for things made by the Gauls, who were the people living in France when the Romans invaded. The Gauls were Celtic people who settled in France about 2,000 years ago.

Some of the oldest **flint tools** in Europe have been found in France. See how many different kinds you can find.

See if you can spot a **bone harpoon,** like this one. They were used for fishing.

You may see a **stone carving** or statue like this. This one is the Venus of Laussel, over 10,000 years old.

The Gauls knew how to work **metal.** This gold disk is very elaborate. Look out for simpler things too.

This **pottery** was made by Gauls in northern France. You will see lots of different shapes.

33

Roman France

Julius Caesar invaded France (or Gaul, as it was called then) in 58BC, and it remained part of the Roman Empire for 400 years. The best Roman remains are in the south, where the climate is like that in Italy.

Roman roads were wide and straight, cutting straight across mountains and rivers. Many modern *Routes Nationales* (main roads) follow the same path. This is the stone foundation of a Roman road.

Towers. Roman towns had strong walls, with towers on them. You can still climb the high Tour Magne at Nîmes.

The only way into a walled town was through its **gateway**. This one is the Porte Auguste at Nîmes.

The Romans put up **monuments to celebrate military victories**. This is the Trophée des Alpes, at La Turbie.

Fortified camps housed the Roman legionaries who kept control of the Empire. The best preserved is at Jublains near Evron. It has a high wall with corner towers.

Roman bridges were the only bridges in France until the 1200s. This is the famous Pont du Gard, part of an aqueduct which carried water for 41km from Uzès to Nîmes

Triumphal arches were built to celebrate the military power of Rome. This one is at Orange.

Mausoleums were built as burial places for grand people. There is a specially good one at St-Rémy.

Obelisks were often the markers around which chariot races were run. You can often see them in town squares.

34

Every Roman city had a **theatre** where plays were acted. This one at Orange is one of the best in Europe, and is particularly famous for the 38m high wall behind the stage. An audience of 7,000 people could watch plays there.

Amphitheatres were where the Romans held chariot races, bull-fights and gladiator fights. In some, you can still go and see bullfights. This one is at Nîmes.

Roman temples were richly carved and decorated. This is the Maison Carrée at Nîmes, a rare example of a Roman building which is not in ruins.

The **Roman town** at Vaison-la-Romaine, near Orange, once had about 20,000 inhabitants. You can see the remains of grand villas, temples and a theatre.

Mosaics like this, made from many small coloured stones, covered the floors of important villas and temples. You will sometimes see them in museums.

Roman ornaments, statues and coins have been dug up all over the south of France. Look for them in local museums.

Look out for French comic strip books about Asterix the Gaul. In them, you can read about the adventures of a village of Gauls who refused to submit to the Romans.

Visiting a Château

There are hundreds of châteaux all over France. Here are some of the most famous ones. They are nearly all in the Loire valley, which is where the French kings liked to go hunting. Most are open to the public, at least during the summer.

Ussé looks like a fairy-tale castle. It is said to have inspired the story of the Sleeping Beauty.

Blois. Took hundreds of years to build. It has a famous staircase and a secret poisons cupboard.

Chenonceaux was built in a lake. You can hire rowing boats there and travel through the grounds on a miniature train.

Chambord has a maze of 365 chimneys you can walk round, and also a carriage museum. It is the largest Loire valley château.

Vaux-le-Vicomte (Essonne). Built for Fouquet, Louis XIV's finance minister, who some people say was the "Man in the Iron Mask". His symbol, a squirrel, is all over the house.

Chaumont. Its name means "hot mountain", and it has pictures of volcanoes on the walls. Also famous for its velvet-lined stables.

Langeais is a fortress château with drawbridge, dungeons and ramparts.

Amboise has a balcony where 1,509 people were hanged in 1560. Nearby is the Clos Lucé museum which has models of da Vinci inventions.

Samur fortress château is the home of the *Cadre Noir* riding school. You can watch the riders practising.

Versailles

Versailles (near Paris) was the home of Louis XIV, XV and XVI. It is said that 5,000 servants were needed to run this château because it is so vast.

Hall of Mirrors. Mirrors were so expensive that you had to be very wealthy to own even one. Louis XIV had a whole room lined with them at Versailles.

There are several small houses in the grounds of Versailles. This one is called the **Petit Trianon.**

The Grand Trianon at Versailles is like a small palace. It was built so the king could escape the formal life of court.

At the **Petit Hameau,** Queen Marie Antoinette played at being a shepherdess, and put bows round the lambs' necks.

Château gardens

At many châteaux, you will see **formal gardens,** which were the fashion in the 17th century. Lakes, fountains, hedges and flowerbeds make a huge pattern.

There is often an **orangery,** where you will see orange trees in tubs. Oranges were used to make the house smell nice in the days before there were proper washing facilities.

Low clipped **box hedges** are used to make patterns. Sometimes the pattern is a royal symbol (see page 41).

Look out for neat **cone-shaped trees** that are so tidy they look artificial. They are real trees, carefully trimmed.

There are often spectacular **fountains.** The Versailles ones are working on some Sundays in summer.

What to Look for in a Château I

The name château means "castle", but, though the early ones have strong defences, most are grand houses built in more peaceful times. Here are some examples of how building styles changed over the years. When you see a château, try to date it from its style.

1000s Square Donjon. Thick stone walls, narrow arrow slits. Entrance on an upper floor.

1100s Round Donjon. Easier to defend than square donjon, because no corners for enemy to hide round.

1200s Donjon surrounded by a courtyard, called a bailey, and a strong stone wall. Sometimes there are two or three baileys and walls.

1300s Final development of fortress château. Large but compact building with inner courtyard, turrets, battlement walks and arrow slits.

1400s Gradual change from fortress to country house. Outer walls still have the look of a fortress, but walls facing courtyard have larger windows, and decoration. Tall roofs.

1500s (Renaissance Style). Corner turrets for decoration only. Dormer windows in roof, decorated chimneys, pillars and open walkways.

Early 1600s (Louis XIII Style). Pink or red brick with white stone facings around windows, doorways and corners. No turrets.

Late 1600s (Early Classical Style). Corner "pavilions" at each end of house. Plainer style, tall roofs – often domed – and larger windows.

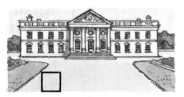

1700s (Classical Style). Less carving and decoration. Lots of windows, flat roof with balustrades and ornamental vases, pillars and columns.

1800s Little that was new, but drew on ideas from past years, and so often a mixture of styles. This house has a tall roof of 1600s and front of 1700s.

Things to spot in châteaux

Here are some things to look out for when you visit a château. Many châteaux were added to and changed over the years, so you are likely to see things built at different times in the same place.

Drawbridge. A bridge across the moat which could be raised when enemies approached.

Watch turrets. Small round rooms sticking out from top of wall, where look-outs could watch for enemies.

Machicolations. Holes below the battlements through which missiles and boiling tar could be dropped on attackers.

Arrow slits. Narrow openings in walls, through which arrows could be shot, while archers remained safe.

Sloping walls at the bottom of towers made it harder for enemies to attack with battering rams and ladders.

Murder holes in the ceiling of the gateway were also for dropping things like boiling tar on to enemies.

Cross bows were the most common weapons in the 1400s. You may see them hung on walls.

Suit of armour. Worn to protect men when they went into battle. Notice how short many of them are.

39

What to Look for in a Château 2

The direction of most **spiral staircases** allows someone defending the stairs from above to have his sword arm free.

Tapestries were used to decorate walls and to keep draughts out. They were often made specially for the house and show Bible scenes, myths or historical events.

Inside walls were often covered with **patterned leather** to keep out the damp.

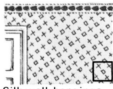

Silk wall-hangings were changed every season. Red in winter, green in spring, white in summer, gold in autumn.

Later châteaux have **painted and moulded wall and door panels.** Lots of gold paint was used.

Painted wooden ceilings with exposed beams and geometric patterns are quite common.

Coffered ceilings have carved and painted wooden panels sunk into a wooden framework. Usually in grand rooms.

Paintings on the ceilings are sometimes by famous artists. Some appear to be three-dimensional.

Four poster beds had thick curtains to keep out draughts and screen the occupants from people passing through the room.

You will sometimes see a **travelling chest** like this, with secret compartments for documents and jewels.

Red Indian heads were carved on the legs of many pieces of furniture after the discovery of America in 1492.

In many châteaux you can see the vast kitchens where meals were prepared for thousands of people. Look out for **copper cooking pans**.

The larger châteaux were like small villages and had everything the occupants needed, including a private **chapel** like this one.

The owners of the château

Look for symbols above doors, windows and fireplaces.

Initials. See how many different ones you can find.

The **family's crest**, in this case a squirrel, may be carved in wood, painted or embroidered on tapestries.

Rich people often had their **portraits** painted so you can see what the former inhabitants looked like.

Symbols of kings and queens

Many kings and queens had their own symbols and you will see them, not only in their own châteaux, but also in those of loyal nobles. Only in royal houses, though, will you see symbols with crowns above them.

A **porcupine** was the symbol of Louis XII (1498–1515).

A **Franciscan girdle with ermine tufts** became Anne of Brittany and Charles VIII's symbol when they married in 1491.

A **salamander** was the crest of François I (1515–1547).

Anne of Brittany and her daughter Claude had an **ermine** as their symbol.

The **Sun King,** Louis XIV, used this symbol (1643–1715).

The Bourbon royal family symbol was the **fleur de lys** (1589–1610).

Churches

Here are some of the different types of church buildings you will see in France. When you visit churches, remember you should wear decent clothes – not shorts or bathing costumes. You can visit a few monasteries, but most prefer you to write and make arrangements first.

Basilica. Modelled on Roman law-court buildings. Usually built over the tomb of a saint.

Baptistery. A separate building from the main church, used for baptizing people into the Christian religion.

Abbey or monastery. Home of a community of monks. An abbey is a monastery ruled by an abbot. The monks were wealthy and powerful in the Middle Ages and were responsible for the building of many churches.

A **cathedral** is a church ruled by a bishop. The bishop's throne used to be called the **cathedra**.

Bridge chapels. Travellers prayed for a safe journey in these. and left money for the upkeep of the bridge.

Fortified churches, which look like castles, were built during the Middle Ages when there were many religious wars.

Rock-pinnacle churches. You will sometimes see churches like this in mountainous regions, like the Auvergne.

Enclosures. You will see these in Brittany. They consist of a triumphal arch leading to a cemetery, a church, an ossuary (where bones are kept) and a calvary, which is a large carved stone cross. Many were built during the plague in 1598.

Domed churches, like those in Eastern Europe, are sometimes found in southern France.

42

Things to spot in churches

Despite many religious wars, the Roman Catholic Church has been strong in France since the Middle Ages. In the 1100s, there was even a pope in France who lived in Avignon. Here are some things to look out for in Roman Catholic churches.

Holy water stoop. On entering a church, people bless themselves by making the sign of the cross with holy water.

Each chapel inside the church is dedicated to a saint. People **light a candle** for each prayer they make to the saint.

Pilgrims still visit churches where there are relics of a saint, in the hope that they will be helped or cured. There are special saints to help with different problems. Holy places like Lourdes are also visited by pilgrims.

Reliquary. A box, shaped like a church or a hollow statue, in which relics, often bones, of a saint are kept.

The **confessional** is a box where people confess their sins to a priest, who cannot see them.

The **choir screen** encloses the choir which is where the priests pray. It is often richly carved.

Misericord. Small carved perch on the back of a choir stall, on which the priests can rest.

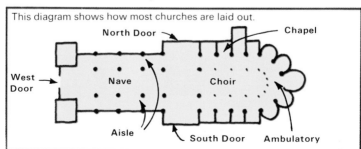

This diagram shows how most churches are laid out.

North Door — Chapel
West Door →
Nave
Choir
Aisle
South Door
Ambulatory

43

Finding out the Age of a Church

Different styles of church building were introduced as technical knowledge increased. Here you can see the main features of each period of architecture. See if you can spot them when you visit a church.

Front view
Back view

Romanesque (1000s–1100s). Builders borrowed many ideas from earlier Roman buildings. Quite squat, with a few small windows set in thick stone walls. Rounded arches on windows, doors and vaults.

Gothic (1100s–1400s). Tall building, many windows, pointed arches. Lots of flying buttresses.

Renaissance (1500s). Use of Italian ideas of architecture. Rounder arches, pillars and ornate decoration.

Classical (1600s). Domed roof rather than tower. Plainer style, straight pillars and windows.

Towers

Romanesque. Low, 8-sided or square. Pyramid roof.

Gothic Tower. Square, often with 8-sided upper level.

Gothic spire. Small square tower, with tall narrow spire.

Renaissance Bell Tower. Small domed top with lantern.

Doorways

Romanesque. Rounded arch with many carvings round it.

Gothic. Pointed arch. Many sculptures. The "tympanum" (space inside arch, above the door) is often carved.

Renaissance. Usually two separate doors under one very high tympanum.

44

Ceilings

Romanesque **barrel vault**. Rounded vault with a series of exposed arches.

Romanesque **oven vault**. A quarter of a sphere forms the roof of the small chapels in the church.

Late Romanesque **groin vault**. Two overlapping barrel vaults. Cannot see the arches.

Gothic **rib vault**. Many tall pointed arches, meeting at a centre point.

Renaissance **lantern vault**. Pendulums hang from the centre of the vault.

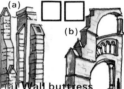

(a) **Wall buttress** presses against outer wall to give support.
(b) **Flying buttress** stands away from wall. Gives even greater support.

Windows

Romanesque. Small rounded arch on top. Side pillars and plain glass.

Early Gothic Lancet style. Narrow, slightly pointed arch.

Radiant Gothic. Tall pointed arch. Circle pattern.

Flamboyant Gothic. Tall pointed arch. Flame-like pattern.

Renaissance. Tall with round arch. Little ironwork decoration.

Rose Wheel

Radiant Rose

Flamboyant Rose

Rose windows are often seen in French Gothic cathedrals, usually above the west door. Their pattern is similar to that of the other windows.

45

Church Decorations

Many churches were built in the days before most people could read or write. They were decorated with pictures in stone or glass, which told stories from the Bible or of the lives of the saints. Here are some examples of where to look for picture stories.

Capitals are at the top of pillars. They are usually carved. Romanesque capitals have designs of leaves, flowers, geometric patterns and often sinister monsters. Gothic capitals have small scenes from the Bible.

Look for **medallions** on either side of the west door. They show:

(a)

(b)

(c)

(a) Virtues and vices. This is the sin of cowardice — an armed man is running from a hare.

(b) Signs of the Zodiac. This is the ram of Aries.

(c) Seasons. Here you can see the harvest time.

Stained glass often has biblical scenes. Usually found only in Gothic or later churches.

Gargoyles on church roofs were supposed to frighten away evil spirits. Also used as rain water spouts.

The saints and martyrs can be recognized by symbols carved on their statues. Here are some to spot.

St Luke (angel)   **St John** (eagle)

St Mark (lion)   **St Matthew** (bull)

St Peter holds the keys of heaven.   **St Paul** holds the sword which killed him.

John the Baptist holds a lamb.

St James has a cockle shell and a pilgrim's staff.

St Sebastian is pierced by arrows.

Painted vaults. Originally churches were completely painted inside. Most of the colours have faded or disappeared now, but you may be lucky and see a ceiling which is still painted.

Frescoes are pictures painted straight onto the wet plaster of the walls. They were often used in churches, especially in the south.

Look out for a **pulpit fixed to the wall.** These often have carvings, or even statues, on the roof. See if you can find a staircase for the priest to climb up.

Dog

Lion

Tombs. A dog at the feet of a figure on a tomb means the person died peacefully. A lion means the person was killed in battle.

See if you can spot an ornate **ironwork bell-cage** on the roof of the church tower, especially in the south of France.

When a **cardinal** died, his **hat** was often hung from the roof of the church. You can still see them sometimes, for instance at Beauvais.

Dead Men's Lantern. Often found near cemeteries in the south-west. The light was to keep watch over the dead, and guide pilgrims on their way.

Coloured stone **mosaics** often decorate the floors of churches. This one, at Chartres Cathedral, shows a maze through which sinners had to walk.

Fun Things to Do 1

Zoos and safari parks

The *Syndicat d'Initiative* (Tourist Office) in the town where you are staying will give you lists of things to see and do nearby. Look out for posters advertising things too. The next few pages suggest what sort of things to look out for.

This is the **Safari Park** at Thot in the Périgord. Here you can see bison, wild boar and other animals similar to those in the prehistoric wall paintings found in the caves of the area.

In the park around the Château de Thoiry-en-Yvelines, 40km west of Paris, you can see over 800 **wild animals** from Africa and Asia roaming free.

There are **bird sanctuaries** in many parts of France. Le Parc Ornithologique at Villars Les Dombes, (Ain) has over 200 species of birds.

At the top of the steps leading to the Royal Palace of Monaco in Monte Carlo, there is a huge **aquarium** full of different varieties of tropical fish.

At the **Marineland Dolphinarium** on the Côte d'Azur you can watch dolphins and a killer whale dance and do acrobatics. The show is floodlit at night.

Adventure playgrounds

In the **deer park** at Jonchery-sur-Vesle, (Aisne) there is a children's adventure playground, where you will find lots of things to play with.

You can become a Red Indian for a day at this **Indian village** in the Vallée des Peaux Rouges (Valley of the Red Indians) north of Paris.

National parks

In each region of France, large areas of beautiful countryside have been turned into *parcs nationaux* (national parks), where the land and animals are protected. Most of the parks are uninhabited and they are good places to go walking, pony-trekking, canoeing, fishing, cycling and rock climbing.

The Camargue is one of the national parks. It is a large area of marshland across the Rhône delta. Lots of animals and birds, such as beavers and flamingoes, live there. The Camargue is famous for its wild, white horses and black bulls. Look out for horsemen carrying pronged sticks rounding them up.

Caves

At the Gouffre du Padirac. Gramat, Lot, you can go on a **boat tour along an underground river** through caves up to 100m high. The caves are illuminated, and you can see gigantic stalactites which are centuries old.

Circuses

Look out for posters advertising travelling **circuses**. You can see performing animals and flying trapeze acts, which were invented by a French acrobat called Léotard in 1859.

Fun Things to Do 2

Highly skilled people still practise many of the traditional crafts in France. Factories and workshops, where you can see how things are made, are often open to the public. Here are some places you can visit.

At the Chocolaterie Poulin, Blois (Loire-et-Cher), you can watch **chocolates** being made.

There are small **potteries** all over France, especially in Provence and Alsace, which you can visit.

At Biot in Provence you can visit the **glassworks** (*verrerie*) to see how glass is blown and cut. Every month they make a different coloured glass.

Le Musée Historique du Papier at Ambert in the Auvergne is really an old **paper factory**. You can watch the traditional methods of making paper by hand.

Grasse, Provence, is the centre of the French **perfume** industry. At the Fragonard factory you can see how the oil for perfume is extracted from flowers.

At Roquefort in the Languedoc you can visit the cellars where the smelly blue-veined **Roquefort cheeses** are left to mature. They are made from ewes' milk.

The Chinon-Richelieu Railway. In the summer you can travel on the small vintage **steam train** from Chinon to the **model village** of Richelieu (Indre-et-Loire).

The **funicular (cable) railway** from St Hilaire-du-Touret in the Savoie climbs up a mountain side and is the steepest climbing railway in Europe.

Wine-making

The main wine producing regions of France are Burgundy, Bordeaux, Alsace, the Rhône and Champagne. Look out for roads through the wine regions marked *Route du Vin*. These take you past the main vineyards. The best time of year to visit them is early autumn.

When you are driving through vineyards, look out for signs saying *Salons de Dégustation* or *Visitez les Caves*. In any of these places you can visit the cellars where the wine is made. You can also taste some of the wines.

Champagne cellars are huge. At Mercier in Épernay there is a small train to take you around them.

In Burgundy people taste wine from a "taste-vin" like this, so they can see its colour more easily.

In the old houses at Riquewihr in Alsace you can see old wine presses and huge, decorated casks.

In the evenings from early summer until the autumn you can see Son et Lumière (Sound and Light) performances at many historic houses and churches. The performance of acting, music and lightshow takes you through the history of the place. Here you can see the Son et Lumière pageant at one of the Loire valley châteaux.

Fun Things to Do 3

There are lots of interesting museums in France. Most areas have a folklore museum, where you can see how people used to live. There are also museums with unusual collections. Here are some ideas for different museums you could visit.

Toy museums

Le Musée du Jouet, Poissy, (Ile de France). In this museum you can see about 500 different **toys and games** from the 1800s. In one room you can even find out how they were made.

Musée National de Monaco. This Museum contains a collection of **clockwork dolls** from the 1700s and 1800s. The dolls are in period costume. You can watch them in action and see a display showing how they were made.

Musée Gadagne, Lyon, (Rhône). In this **puppet museum** you can see the history of the famous Guignol puppets, the French version of Punch and Judy.

Musée d'Allard, Montbrison, (Loire). This collection shows the history of **dolls** from all over the world. The oldest doll is over 3000 years old.

Musée de Champlitte, (Haute-Saône). Reconstructed **interiors of houses,** farms and shops show you how people once lived in this region of France.

Musée Basque, Bayonne, is a **folklore museum.** It has interiors of local houses, farm machines, costumes and games.

Transport museums

Musée de l'Automobile, Le Mans, (Sarthe). On the famous 24 hour race track at Le Mans you can see a collection of 140 **cars** made between 1884 and 1970.

Château Lannessan, Cussac, Aquitaine. This is a museum of **horse-drawn vehicles.** You can see carriages and harnesses and visit the old stables.

Le Musée de l'Automobile, Rochetaillée-sur-Saône. This museum has a collection of **vintage cars** which are still in good working order.

Balloon Museum, Balleroy, Normandy. In this museum you can trace the history of **hot-air balloons** and see how they work.

Other interesting museums

Musée des Beaux Arts, Besançon. In the clock department of this museum you can see old **clocks,** sundials and the most complicated watch in the world.

Musée du Phonographe, Sainte-Maxime (Var). Here you can trace the history of **gramophones** and see many old barrel organs, pianolas and musical boxes.

The **Bayeux tapestry** is in a house next to the cathedral at Bayeux in Normandy. The tapestry is 70m long and shows, in 58 brightly coloured scenes, how William the Conqueror invaded England in 1066. It used to hang in Bayeux Cathedral and was probably embroidered in England.

Sports

If you are interested in sport, there are lots of things you can see or do while you are in France. All French towns have good sports facilities in their *Stade Municipale,* and anyone can use them at low cost. Here are some sports you can watch or try yourself.

Cycling is a good way to explore an area you do not know. You can hire bicycles from the railway station in most towns and from some cycle shops. Remember to ride on the right and give way to traffic coming from the right.

The French play **tennis** all the year round. The tourist office will give you a list of tennis courts you can hire in the area where you are staying.

Ice skating is popular in France and you can go skating in most towns. You will be able to hire skates at the ice rink, which is called *la patinoire.*

In the winter you can go **cross-country skiing** *(ski-de-fond)* in hilly areas. It is great fun and you do not need any experience.

Amateur, 15-a-side **rugby union** is popular in France, especially in Aquitaine and Languedoc. You can watch matches every Saturday during the winter.

You can watch **soccer** matches in most towns every Saturday from August to May. The French Cup Final, the highlight of the season, is held in Paris in June.

The big sporting events

The **24 Heures du Mans** is a 24 hour car race at Le Mans, Sarthe. It is one of the most famous car races in the world and takes place at the end of spring every year.

The **Monte Carlo Rally** is held every January. Rally drivers set off from all over Europe and meet in the South of France to race through the streets of Monte Carlo, in Monaco.

The **Tour de France** is a cycling race round France, which begins in June and ends in July. The route is split into 22 laps and covers about 4,000km. It ends in Paris.

The **Prix de l'Arc de Triomphe** is a famous horse race, which is held every autumn at the Longchamp race track outside Paris. The prize money is the highest in Europe for a horse race.

Festivals and Carnivals 1

There are many festivals in France. Some celebrate religious occasions, others historical events or even just a good harvest. Here are some of the special festivals and traditions.

On 14 July everyone in France celebrates the storming of the Bastille prison at the beginning of the French Revolution. Houses are decorated with flags and garlands, there are torchlit processions, military parades and firework displays, and people dance in the streets until dawn.

On **Christmas Eve** children put out shoes, rather than stockings, for Father Christmas to fill with gifts.

The traditional **Christmas** pudding is the Bûche de Noël, a cake shaped like a yule log and coated in chocolate.

In Provence, people take live lambs to church at **Christmas** time and lay them at the foot of the crib.

On **6 December** people in the north and east of France celebrate the Fête de St Nicolas (Santa Claus), the patron saint of children. In many towns you can see a man dressed as a bishop walking through the streets with a donkey and handing out sweets and chocolates to children.

At midnight on **New Year's Eve** (Saint-Sylvestre), people in cars all sound their car horns as loudly as they can to celebrate the new year.

On **6 January** the French celebrate la Fête des Rois (festival of the three kings). People eat a special cake, and the person who finds the bean hidden in it is King of the Day.

After a **Christening** the guests and children outside the church are given small bags of pink or blue sugared almonds, called dragées.

In villages, especially on Saturdays, you might see a **bride and groom** walking down the street with children holding flowers above their heads.

On special days like Christmas, there are often **skiing displays** in the mountains. Ski guides ski down the mountains at night carrying flaming torches.

In northern France huge models of local historical or legendary heroes, called **Les Géants** (the giants) are paraded through the streets on festive occasions.

Festivals and Carnivals 2

The **carnival at Nice** is the biggest in France. It lasts for 12 days and ends on Shrove Tuesday (le Mardi Gras). The whole town is lit up and people line the streets to watch colourful processions go by. You can join in a battle of flowers with the people on floats and watch fireworks being let off over the sea.

On **1 May** people give their friends bunches of lilies of the valley, to bring them good luck.

Flower festivals, like the Jasmin Festival at Grasse, are held in all the big flower-growing areas in the summer. Floats covered with flowers file through the streets, and people throw flowers at each other.

Many areas in France have their own special **religious festivals.** You may see processions of pilgrims in traditional costume.

On the **Pfiffertag** (piper's day) in Ribeauvillé, Alsace, people in traditional costume dance through the streets of the village carrying a giant cake.

Les Vendanges (grape harvest). In the big wine producing areas the local people celebrate the end of the grape harvest every autumn. They hold big dances and taste the new wine. Members of the old wine societies dress up in their traditional costume.

Basque Festivals. The Basque region in south-west France has special traditions of its own. All through the year you can go to lively festivals of Basque dancing and watch traditional hobby-horse and sword dances.

Bullfighting. A lot of bulls are bred in the South of France and you can go to bull fights in towns such as Nîmes and Arles. In the summer you can also watch bull-chasing, which is very popular and where the bulls are not killed.

Many towns have **fun fairs** during the summer with fireworks and decorated floats. You will see posters advertising them. Look on page 61 for the French words for fair and fireworks. At Chinon, in the Loire valley, in August, there is a medieval festival with acrobats, jugglers and fire-eaters.

Car Number-Plate Game

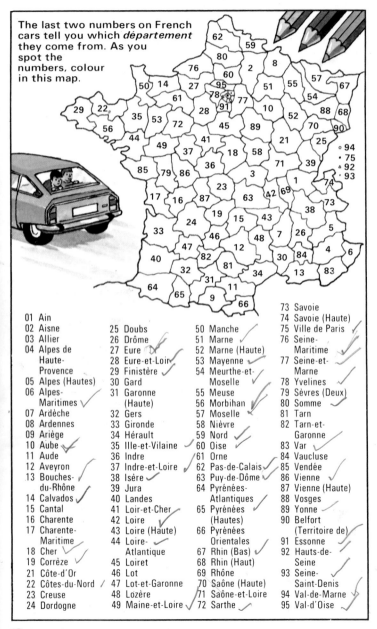

The last two numbers on French cars tell you which *département* they come from. As you spot the numbers, colour in this map.

01 Ain
02 Aisne
03 Allier
04 Alpes de Haute-Provence
05 Alpes (Hautes)
06 Alpes-Maritimes
07 Ardèche
08 Ardennes
09 Ariège
10 Aube
11 Aude
12 Aveyron
13 Bouches-du-Rhône
14 Calvados
15 Cantal
16 Charente
17 Charente-Maritime
18 Cher
19 Corrèze
21 Côte-d'Or
22 Côtes-du-Nord
23 Creuse
24 Dordogne

25 Doubs
26 Drôme
27 Eure
28 Eure-et-Loir
29 Finistère
30 Gard
31 Garonne (Haute)
32 Gers
33 Gironde
34 Hérault
35 Ille-et-Vilaine
36 Indre
37 Indre-et-Loire
38 Isère
39 Jura
40 Landes
41 Loir-et-Cher
42 Loire
43 Loire (Haute)
44 Loire-Atlantique
45 Loiret
46 Lot
47 Lot-et-Garonne
48 Lozère
49 Maine-et-Loire

50 Manche
51 Marne
52 Marne (Haute)
53 Mayenne
54 Meurthe-et-Moselle
55 Meuse
56 Morbihan
57 Moselle
58 Nièvre
59 Nord
60 Oise
61 Orne
62 Pas-de-Calais
63 Puy-de-Dôme
64 Pyrénées-Atlantiques
65 Pyrénées (Hautes)
66 Pyrénées Orientales
67 Rhin (Bas)
68 Rhin (Haut)
69 Rhône
70 Saône (Haute)
71 Saône-et-Loire
72 Sarthe

73 Savoie
74 Savoie (Haute)
75 Ville de Paris
76 Seine-Maritime
77 Seine-et-Marne
78 Yvelines
79 Sèvres (Deux)
80 Somme
81 Tarn
82 Tarn-et-Garonne
83 Var
84 Vaucluse
85 Vendée
86 Vienne
87 Vienne (Haute)
88 Vosges
89 Yonne
90 Belfort (Territoire de)
91 Essonne
92 Hauts-de-Seine
93 Seine-Saint-Denis
94 Val-de-Marne
95 Val-d'Oise

Useful Addresses

The French Government Tourist Office (FGTO) will supply lists of hotels and campsites and details of tours. They also provide booklets on each region of France, and the addresses of local tourist offices.
If you speak some French, ask for a booklet called *Loisirs en France.* This tells you many interesting things you can do on holiday in France.
French Government Tourist Office, 178 Piccadilly, London W1V 0AL. tel: (01) 491 2516.

For general information on France, contact the Cultural Service of the French Embassy.
French Embassy (Cultural Service), 22 Wilton Crescent, London SW1. tel: (01) 235 8080.

Where to stay and how to get there

The Youth Hostels Association and the books listed below will also tell you where you can stay.
Youth Hostels Association (YHA), 14 Southampton Street, London WC2. tel: (01) 836 8541.
French Farm and Village Holiday Guide (Duo Publishing).
Campsites in France (Letts).

For general information on travelling in France, contact a travel agent or the French Railways, or look out for the Michelin maps listed below.
French Railways, 179 Piccadilly, London W1V 0BA. tel: (01) 493 9731/4451.
989 France (road map)
915 France Main Roads/Atlas
400 France Motorways/Atlas.

Guide books and phrase books

The Michelin green tourist guides are probably the best basic guide books to France. Each one deals with a different region and gives you general information about the area, as well as suggesting interesting places to visit and good routes to take. Some other guide books are listed below.
   You will have much more fun on holiday if you can speak some French. You will find a phrase book very useful.
Letts go to France (Letts).
The Young Traveller's Guide to France (Duo Publishing).
French Riviera (Berlitz).
Loire Valley (Berlitz).
Junior Guide to French (Usborne)

Some useful French words

castle
le château
ler shattoh
church
l'église
leggleez
circus
le cirque
ler seerk
exhibition
l'exposition
lekspozeesyong
fair
la fête foraine
lah fet foren
fireworks
les feux d'artifice
lay fer darteefeess

flea market
le marché aux puces
ler marshay oh pewss
glassworks
la verrerie
lah vairereee
guide book
le guide
ler geed
market
le marché
ler marshay
monastery
le monastère
ler monastair
museum
le musée
ler mewzay

park
le jardin public
ler jardang pewbleek
pottery
la poterie
lah potree
swimming pool
la piscine
lah peeseen
tennis court
le terrain de tennis
ler terrang der teneess
wine cellars
les caves
lay kahv
zoo
le jardin zoologique
ler jardang zo-olojeek

Index

62

64

Part 2

FRENCH PHRASES

and how to say them

Contents of Part 2

How to Use this Part of the Book

This book will help you make yourself understood in most everyday situations when you are on holiday or travelling in France. The phrases have been kept as simple as possible, and include some of the possible answers to the questions you may want to ask. There are also translations of many of the signs you will see.

The book is divided into sections, each covering a situation you are likely to find yourself in. Use the contents list at the front or the index at the back to help you find the pages you need. You will find it easier if you look up the section you are going to need in advance, so you can practise saying the phrases.

For most phrases, there is a picture with a speech bubble containing the French. Underneath the picture is a guide to help you pronounce the French and an English translation. Like this:

Je parle français.

Jer parl fronsay.
I can speak French.

On the next two pages, you will find out how to use the pronunciation guide and there are some useful hints and phrases to remember. At the back of the book, there are a few common verbs and some very basic French grammar.

Points to remember

We have not always had enough space to include the words for "please" (*s'il vous plaît*). Try to remember to add them when you are asking for things.

S'il vous plaît

There are two words in French for "you"—*vous* and *tu*. *Tu* is used by close friends and children. Be careful about using *tu,* because people will think you rude if you say it to someone you don't know very well. We have used *vous* in this book, except where the conversation is between children as, for instance, in the section on "Making Friends".

Tu or Vous?

Pronunciation Guide

We have tried to keep the pronunciation guides in this book as simple as possible. For each French sound, we have used the English word, or part of a word, which sounds most like it. Read the pronunciation guide in what seems to be the most obvious way and try not to stress one syllable more than another. It will sound better if you say it quickly, so it is a good idea to practise a bit. People should be able to understand what you are saying, even if you won't sound quite like a French person. If you want to learn really good pronunciation you should try to find a French person to teach you.

Here are some general points to remember when you are trying to speak French.

The French "j" has a soft sound, like the sound in the middle of the English word "leisure". Whenever you see a "j" in the pronunciation guide you should say it in this way.

Many French words have a "nasal" ("nose-y") sound which we do not have in English. We have used "ong" and "ang" for this in the pronunciation guide.

When you are saying this, do not stress the "g". It should almost not be there.

The French "r" should be rolled at the back of the throat, rather like the sound you make when you gargle. See if you can do it. If you can't, don't worry, people will still be able to understand you.

In French, "h" is silent, so when you see one in a French word just ignore it.

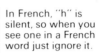

Consonants (that is, all letters except a, e, i, o and u) at the ends of words are not usually pronounced, as in *l'aéroport* (airport), which is pronounced lairo-por.

You will see four different kinds of accents when you are reading French words. An "e" at the end of the word is not pronounced unless it has an acute accent on top, like this, "é". Then you pronounce it as "ay"

The French "u" is pronounced like the "ew" in the English word "dew". We have used "ew" for it in the pronunciation guide. For example:

allumettes (matches)
= allewmett

Some Basic Words and Phrases

Here are some useful words and phrases which you will need in all kinds of situations.

Oui
Wee
Yes

Non
Nong
No

S'il vous plaît
Seelvooplay
Please

Merci
Mairsee
Thank you

Bonjour
Bongjoor
Hello

Au revoir
Orvwar
Goodbye

Pardon
Pardong
I'm sorry

Excusez-moi
Exkewzay-mwah
Excuse me

Monsieur
Moosyer
Mr

Madame
Madarm
Mrs

Mademoiselle
Madmwazell
Miss

Some simple questions

How much or many?	Combien? Combeeyen?
Why?	Pourquoi? Poorkwah?
Which one?	Lequel or Laquelle? Lerkell or lahkell?
Where is...?	Où est...? Oo ay...?
When?	Quand? Kong?
Have you...?	Avez-vous...? Avay-voo...?
Is or are there...?	Y a-t-il...? Ee ateel...?

Some simple statements

I am	Je suis... Jer swee...
I have...	J'ai... Jay...
It is...	C'est... Say...
It is here.	C'est ici. Set ee-see.
It is there.	C'est là. Say lah.
Over there.	Là-bas Lah-bah
This one	Celui-ci Sirlwee-see
That one	Celui-là Sirlwee-lah
I would like...	Je voudrais.. Jer voodray..

Problems with the language

Do you speak English?
Parlez-vous anglais?
Parlay-voo onğ-glay?

I do not speak French.
Je ne parle pas français.
Jer ner parl pah fronsay.

I do not understand.
Je ne comprends pas.
Jer ner comprong pah.

Please speak more slowly.
Plus lentement, s'il vous plaît.
Plew lonte-mong, seelvooplay.

What does that mean?
Qu'est-ce que cela veut dire?
Kessker sirlah ver deer?

Finding Your Way

Pour la gare, s'il vous plaît?

Poor lah gahr, seelvooplay?
How do I get to the railway station, please?

Il faut prendre l'autobus numéro 6.

Eel foe prondr lohtohbewss newmairoh seess.
You must take a number 6 bus.

Où est l'arrêt de l'autobus pour Versailles?

Là-bas. C'est celui-là.

Oo ay larray der lohtohbewss poor Vairsigh?
Where is the bus-stop for Versailles?

Lah bah. Say sirlwee lah.
Over there. It's that one.

Dois-je descendre ici pour Versailles?

Dwarj dessondr ee-see poor Vairsigh?
Is this where I get off for Versailles?

Où est le château, s'il vous plaît?

Oo ay ler shattoh, seelvooplay?
Where is the castle, please?

Je suis perdu. Quel est le nom de cette rue?

Jer swee pairdew. Kell ay ler nom der set rew?
I'm lost. What is the name of this street?

Pouvez-vous me la montrer sur le plan?

Poovay voo mer lah montray syoor ler plong?
Can you show me on the map.

General directions

Tournez à droite.
Toornay ah drwut.
Turn right.

Tournez à gauche.
Toornay ah goash.
Turn left.

Continuez tout droit.
Conteenew-ay too drwuh.
Go straight on.

C'est en face du cinéma.
Set ong fass dew
seenaymah.
**It's opposite the
cinema.**

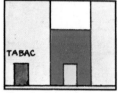

C'est à côté du tabac.
Set ah coatay dew
tabah.
**It's next to the
tobacconists.**

C'est au coin de la rue.
Set oh cwang der lah rew.
It's on the corner.

C'est juste après le pont.
Say joost appray ler pong.
It's just after the bridge.

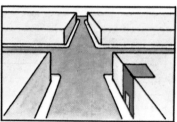

C'est juste avant le carrefour.
Say joost avong ler carrfoor.
It's just before the crossroads.

Some places
to ask for

la gare
lah gahr
railway station.

l'aéroport
lairohpor
airport

la gendarmerie
lah jondarmeree
police station

la banque
lah bonk
bank

les magasins
lay magazang
the shops

At the Railway Station

Oo esskon ashett lay beeyay?
Where can I buy a ticket?

Lah bah, oh geeshay.
Over there, at the ticket office.

Say combeeyen poor Paree?
How much is it to Paris?

Urn beeyay sampl poor Paree.
One single ticket to Paris.

Durr beeyay allay-retoor poor Paree.
Two return tickets to Paris.

Der kell kay par ler trang poor Paree?
Which platform does the Paris train leave from?

Kay newmairoh sank.
Platform 5.

Ah kell urr par ler trang?
What time does the train leave?

C'est bien le train pour Paris?

Say beeyen ler trang poor Paree?
Is this the Paris train?

J'ai perdu mon billet!

Jay pairdew mong beeyay!
I've lost my ticket!

A quelle heure arrive le train de Calais?

Ah kell urr arreev ler trang der Callay?
What time does the train from Calais arrive?

Porteur!

Porturr!
Porter!

Information

Luggage collection

Waiting room

Lost property

Main line trains   **District line trains**

Left luggage

Not drinking water

Do not lean out of the window

Travelling by Car

Où est le garage le plus proche?

Oo ay ler gararj ler plew prosh?
Where is the nearest garage?

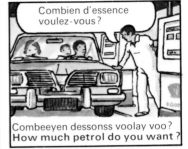

Combien d'essence voulez-vous?

Combeeyen dessonss voolay voo?
How much petrol do you want?

Le plein, s'il vous plaît.

Ler plan, seelvooplay.
Fill it up please.

Pouvez-vous vérifier l'huile et l'eau?

Poovay voo vayreefeeyay lweel ay low?
Can you check the oil and the water?

Je suis en panne.

Jer sweez ong pann.
I have broken down.

Qu'est-ce qui ne va pas?

Kesskee ner vah pah?
What's the trouble?

Les freins ne marchent pas bien.

Lay fran ner marshong pas beeyen.
The brakes are not working properly.

VOITURES DE LOCATION

Je voudrais louer une voiture pour la semaine, s'il vous plaît.

Jer voodray loo-ay ewn vwut-yoor poor lah sirmen, seelvooplay.
I would like to hire a car for the week, please.

Parts of the car

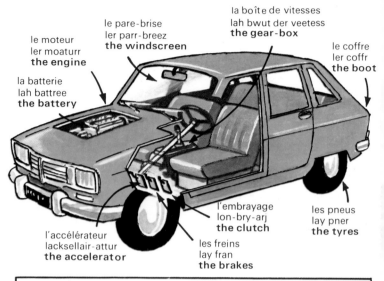

la boîte de vitesses
lah bwut der veetess
the gear-box

le pare-brise
ler parr-breez
the windscreen

le moteur
ler moaturr
the engine

le coffre
ler coffr
the boot

la batterie
lah battree
the battery

l'embrayage
lon-bry-arj
the clutch

les pneus
lay pner
the tyres

l'accélérateur
lacksellair-attur
the accelerator

les freins
lay fran
the brakes

Road signs

Found in forests and dry areas. Warns of the danger of fire.

You have the right of way over cars coming in from side roads.

You no longer have the right of way.

Restricted parking area. Must have a permit, or "Disque Bleue".

Motorway toll 1,000m away.

Entrance to car-park.

TOUTES DIRECTIONS

Means all through traffic should go this way.

Centre Ville

Town centre this way.

Speed limit and end of speed limit signs. Don't forget the numbers are in kilometres.

At the Hotel

A list of recommended hotels and their prices can be obtained from the local tourist office *(Syndicat d'Initiative)*. When staying overnight, you must register with the police. The hotel will usually keep your passport a short while and do this for you.

Booking in advance

Je voudrais réserver une chambre pour la semaine prochaine.

Jer voodray raysairvay ewn shombr poor lah sirmen proshenn.
I would like to book a room for next week.

Finding a room

Je suis désolé, mais l'hôtel est complet.

Jer swee dezolay, may lotel ay complay.
I'm sorry, but the hotel is full.

Est-ce que vous pouvez me conseiller un autre hôtel?

Essker voo poovay mer consayay urn ohtr otel?
Can you recommend another hotel?

Une chambre à deux lits.

Ewn shombr ah durr lee.
A room with two beds.

Une chambre pour deux personnes, avec salle de bain.

Ewn shombr poor durr pairsonn aveck sall der bang.
A double room with bathroom.

Une chambre pour une personne avec douche.

Ewn shombr poor ewn pairson aveck doosh.
A single room with shower.

Vous comptez rester combien de temps?

Voo contay restay combeeyen der tong?
How long will you be staying?

Hotel meals

TARIF

Chambre avec petit déjeuner
Bed and breakfast

Demi-pension
Half board

Pension complète
Full board

A quelle heure servez-vous le petit déjeuner (déjeuner, dîner)?

Ah kell urr sairvay-voo ler pertee dayjernay (dayjernay, deenay)?
What time is breakfast (lunch, dinner) served?

Oeuf sur le plat
Urf syoor ler plah
Fried egg

Oeuf à la coque
Urf ah lah cock
Boiled egg

Oeufs brouillés
Urf breweeyay
Scrambled eggs

Croissant
Cwassong
Flaky roll

Pourriez-vous me faire un pique-nique?

Pooreeyay voo mer fair urn peek-neek?
Could you make me a packed lunch?

Ma clef, s'il vous plaît.

Quel est le numéro de votre chambre?

Mah clay, seal voo play.
My key, please.

Kell ay ler newmairoh der vottr shombr?
What is your room number?

Je voudrais laisser un message pour mon frère.

Jer voodray laysay urn messarj poor mon frair.
I would like to leave a message for my brother.

Paying the bill

Voulez-vous me préparer la note, s'il vous plaît?

Voolay-voo mer preparay lah nott seal voo play?
My bill, please.

Going Camping

Campsites are graded and given from one to four stars. The four star camps are highly organized with many facilities. You can hire caravans, tents or chalets at some camps. You should book in advance if you will be camping during July or August.

Finding a campsite

Peut-on camper ici ?

Pert-ong compay ee-see ?
May we camp here ?

Est-ce qu'il y a un terrain de camping près d'ici ?

Esskeel ya urn terang der comping pray dee-see ?
Is there a campsite near here ?

Nous avons une caravane et deux tentes.

Noozavong ewn caravan ay durr taunt.
We have a caravan and two tents.

At the campsite

Nous voudrions rester quinze jours.

Noo voodreeong restay kanz joor.
We would like to stay a fortnight.

Avez-vous un endroit plus ombragé ?

Avay voo urn ondrwah plooz ombrarjay ?
Have you a shadier place ?

Y a-t-il d'autres familles anglaises ici ?

Ee ateel doetr fameey ong-glairz ee-see ?
Are there any other English families here ?

A quelle heure fermez-vous le soir ?

Ah kell urr fairmay voo ler swar ?
What time do you close in the evenings ?

Où est-ce que je peux me laver?

Ooessker jer per mer lavay?
Where can I wash?

Où est-ce que je peux trouver de l'eau?

Oo essker jer per troovay de low?
Where can I find some water?

Est-ce que je peux emprunter votre lampe de poche?

Essker jer per omprantay vottr lomp der posh?
May I borrow your torch?

Est-ce que c'est permis de faire un feu de camp?

Essker say pairmee der fair urn fur der comp?
Are we allowed to make a camp fire?

Quelle est cette odeur?

Kell ay set ohdurr?
What is that smell?

Pourriez-vous faire un peu moins de bruit, s'il vous plaît?

Pooreeyay voo fair urn per mwan der brwee, sealvooplay?
Please could you make less noise?

What the signs mean

DÉFENSE DE LAVER LA VAISSELLE DANS LES LAVABOS.
No washing up in the basins.

PARKING OBLIGATOIRE
Compulsory parking

EAU POTABLE
Drinking water

RESERVÉ AUX CARAVANES
Caravans only

MESSIEURS LES CAMPEURS SONT PRIÉS DE DÉPOSER LEURS ORDURES DANS LES ENDROITS PRÉVUS À CET EFFET.
Campers are requested to dispose of their rubbish in the places provided.

Going Shopping

Shops are generally open from 8.00 a.m. to 7.00 p.m. Most close on Sundays and many also on Mondays. On the next pages, you can find out where to buy different things. Remember that metric weights and measures are used.

Où puis-je acheter des fruits?

Oo pweej ashtay day frwee?
Where can I buy some fruit?

Avez-vous des pommes?

Avay-voo day pomm?
Have you any apples?

Combien en voudriez-vous?

Un kilo.

Combeeyen ong voodreeay-voo?
How many would you like?

Urn keelo.
A kilo.

Quatre tranches de jambon, s'il vous plaît.

Kattr tronsh der jombong, sealvooplay.
Four slices of ham, please.

Je regarde seulement.

Jer regard sirlmong.
I am just looking.

Signs

Sale

Libre Service

Self Service

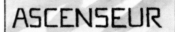

ASCENSEUR

Lifts

Ouvert de 9h à 18.30h

Open from 9 a.m. to 6.30 p.m.

Buying clothes

Pouvez-vous m'aider? Je cherche une chemise imprimée.

Oui. Quelle taille voulez-vous?

Poovay-voo mayday? Jer shairsh ewn shermeez ampreemay.
Can you help me? I am looking for a patterned shirt.

Wee.Kell tye voolay-voo?
Yes. What size do you want?

Puis-je l'essayer?

Pweej lessayay?
May I try it on?

C'est trop grand.
Say troh grong.
It's too big.

C'est trop petit.
Say troh pertee.
It's too small.

C'est trop large.
Say troh larj.
It's too loose.

C'est trop serré.
Say troh serray.
It's too tight.

Ça fait combien?

Sa fay combeeyen?
How much is it?

Avez-vous quelque chose de moins cher?

Avay-voo kellker showz der mwang shair?
Have you anything cheaper?

Où dois-je payer?

Oo dwarj payay?
Where should I pay?

Merci.

Je vous en prie.

Mairsee.
Thank you.

Jer vooz ong pree.
You are welcome.

The Shops 1

ÉPICERIE - ALIMENTATION
Épeesseree-Alleemong-tasseeong
Grocers

Je voudrais . . .

Jer voodray . . .
I would like . . .

des conserves
day konsairv
some tinned foods

du fromage
dew fromarj
some cheese

du beurre
dew burr
some butter

des œufs
dez ur
some eggs

de la confiture
der lah konfeetyoor
some jam

du thé
dew tay
some tea

du lait
dew lay
some milk

du sucre
dew syookr
some sugar

des biscuits
day bee-skwee
biscuits

du miel
dew mee-el
some honey

de la moutarde
der lah mootard
some mustard

du café
dew caffay
some coffee

des haricots verts
dez arreecoe vair
some green beans

des petits pois
day pertee pwah
some peas

un chou-fleur
urn shoo-flurr
a cauliflower

des pommes de terre
day pomm der tair
some potatoes

une laitue
ewn laytew
a lettuce

des champignons
day shompeenyon
some mushrooms

un chou
urn shoo
a cabbage

des tomates
day tomart
some tomatoes

des oignons
dez oy-nyong
some onions

des framboises
day frombwarz
some raspberries

des pommes
day pomm
some apples

des poires
day pwar
some pears

une orange
ewn oranj
an orange

un citron
urn seetrong
a lemon

des fraises
day frairz
some strawberries

des reines-claudes
day renn-clode
some greengages

des prunes
day proon
some plums

82

BOUCHERIE

Boosheree
Butcher

du hachis de bœuf
dew ashee der berf
some minced beef

un poulet
urn poolay
a chicken

un bifteck
urn beefteck
a steak

des escalopes de veau
dez escallopp der voe
some veal escalopes

des côtelettes d'agneau
day cottlett da-nyoh
some lamb chops

Charcuterie

Sharkewtree
Pork Butcher

des saucisses
day sohseess
some sausages

des côtelettes de porc
day cottlett der porr
some pork chops

du pâté
dew pattay
some paté

du saucisson
dew sohseesong
some salami

des hors-d'oeuvres
dez orr durrvr
**some prepared salads
and cooked meats**

BOULANGERIE

Boolonjeree
Baker

des brioches
day breeosh
some sweet rolls

du pain
dew pang
some bread

une baguette
ewn bagett
a long loaf

PATISSERIE-CONFISERIE

Pateeseree-Konfeeseree
Cake and Sweet Shop

une tarte aux fruits
ewn tart oh frwee
a fruit tart

un gâteau
urn gattoh
a cake

des bonbons
day bongbong
some sweets

POISSONNERIE

Pwussonneree
Fishmonger

une sôle
ewn soal
a sole

des crevettes
day krevett
some prawns

un poisson de la région
urn pwahsonn der lah ray-jeeong
a local kind of fish

du cabillaud
dew kabee-yoh
some cod

The Shops 2

Librairie • Papeterie • Maison de la Presse

Leebrairee - Papeeteree - Mayzong der lah Press
Bookshop - Stationers - Newspaper Shop

de l'encre
der lonckr
some ink

un stylo
urn steelo
a pen

un livre
urn leevr
a book

du papier à lettres
dew papeeyay ah lettr
some writing paper

un journal
urn joor-nal
a newspaper

une gomme
ewn gomm
a rubber

un crayon
urn crayong
a pencil

TABAC

Tabah
Tobacconist

des enveloppes
dez onvelopp
some envelopes

un briquet
urn breekay
a lighter

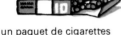

un paquet de cigarettes
urn packay der seegarett
a packet of cigarettes

des allumettes
des allewmett
some matches

des timbres
day tamb
some stamps

boutique de vêtements

Booteek der Vettmong
Clothes Shop

un short
urn short
some shorts

un chapeau
urn shappoh
a hat

une chemise
ewn shermeez
a shirt

une jupe
ewn jyoop
a skirt

une robe
ewn robb
a dress

un pull- ver
urn poolovair
a jersey

des chaussures
day showsyoor
some shoes

des sandales
day sondarl
some sandals

un maillot de bain
urn my-oh der bang
a bathing costume

un imperméable
urn ampairmay-arbl
a raincoat

un pantalon
urn pontalong
some trousers

des collants
day collong
some tights

QUINCAILLERIE·DROGUERIE

Kye-n-kye-eree-Drogree
Ironmongers-Hardware Store

un ouvre-boîtes
urn oovr-bwut
a tin opener

une lampe de poche
ewn lomp der posh
a torch

un tournevis
urn toornvees
a screwdriver

un tire-bouchon
urn teer-booshong
a corkscrew

une pile
ewn peel
a battery

une ampoule
ewn ompool
a light bulb

de la ficelle
der lah feessell
some string

de la lessive
der lah lesseev
some detergent

des ciseaux
day seezoh
some scissors

une aiguille
ewn aygwee
a needle

du coton
dew cotong
some cotton

une prise
ewn preese
a plug

du gaz de camping
dew gaz der compeeng
some Camping Gas

Pharmacie

Farmassee **Chemist**

de l'insecticide
der lanseck-tee-seed
some insect repellent

du savon
dew savong
some soap

de l'aspirine
der laspee-reen
some aspirin

une bande
ewn bond
a bandage

de la crème antiseptique
der lah crem anteesepteek
some antiseptic cream

du talc
dew talk
some talcum powder

du dentifrice
dew donteefreess
some toothpaste

une brosse à dents
ewn bross ah dong
a toothbrush

une pellicule
ewn pelleckewl
a film

des sparadraps
day sparadrah
some sticking plasters

un peigne
urn penn
a comb

du papier hygiénique
dew papeeyay eejee-ayneek
some toilet paper

Posting a Letter . . .

The post office is called the P.T.T. *(Postes, Télégraphes, Téléphones)*. They are usually open from 8.00 a.m. to 7.00 p.m. on weekdays, and from 8.00 a.m. to midday on Saturdays. Stamps can also be bought from a café-tabac. Post boxes are usually yellow.

Quel est le prix d'un timbre pour une carte postale pour l'Angleterre?

Kelly ay ler pree durn tambr poor ewn cart postarl poor long-gletair?
How much is a stamp for a postcard to England?

Je voudrais quatre timbres pour l'Angleterre.

Jer voodray kattr tambr poor long-gletair.
I would like four stamps for England.

Où puis-je trouver une boîte aux lettres?

Oo pweej troovay ewn bwut oh lettr?
Where can I find a postbox?

The post office

Où est le bureau principal des P.T.T. s'il vous plaît?

Oo ay ler bewroh pranseepal day Pay Tay Tay, sealvooplay?
Where is the main post office, please?

TÉLÉGRAMMES

Je voudrais envoyer un télégramme en Angleterre.

Jer voodray onvwye-ay urn taylaygram on ong-gletair.
I would like to send a telegram to England.

Remplissez cette fiche, s'il vous plaît.

Rompleesay set feesh, sealvooplay.
Fill in this form please.

Quel est le prix par mot?

Kell ay ler pree par mow?
How much is it per word?

. . . and Changing Money

Il coûte combien pour envoyer ce paquet à l'Angleterre ?

Eel coot combeeyen poor onvwye-ay sir packay ah long-gletair ?
How much will it cost to send this parcel to England ?

A quelle heure a lieu la dernière levée de courrier ?

Ah kell urr ah lyer lah dairnee-air lervay der cooree-ay ?
What time does the last post leave ?

Signs

TÉLÉGRAMMES

Telegrams

TIMBRES POSTE

Postage stamps

PAR AVION

Air mail

PAQUETS

Parcels

JETONS

Telephone tokens

Changing money

Traveller's cheques can be changed in a bank, a *Bureau de Change* or in some officially authorized hotels. Banks are open from 9.00 a.m. to midday and from 2.00 p.m. to 4.30 p.m. In country areas they may open on only a few days.

Puis-je encaisser un chèque de voyage ici ?

Pweej onkessay urn sheck der vwye-arj ee-see ?
Can I cash a traveller's cheque here ?

Combien vaut la livre ?

Combeeyen voh lah leevr ?
How many francs are there to the pound ?

Pourriez-vous me donner de la monnaie ?

Pooree-ay voo mer donnay der lah monnay ?
Could I have some small change ?

Going to a Café

Cafés stay open from early in the morning to very late at night. They serve snack meals and both alcoholic and non-alcoholic drinks. It is cheaper if you stand inside at the bar than if you sit at a table. Many cafés have pinball machines inside.

Est-ce que cette table est occupée?

Essker set tarbl ett ockewpay?
Is this table taken?

Qu'est-ce que je vous sers, Messieurs?

Kessker jer voo sair, Messyer?
What can I get you?

Je voudrais voir la carte, s'il vous plaît.

Jer voodray vwar lah cart, seelvoo-play.
I would like to see the menu, please.

Qu'est-ce que vous avez comme sandwichs?

Jambon, fromage et saucisson.

Kessker vooz avay comm sondweech?
What sandwiches have you got?
Jombong, fromarj ay sohseesong.
Ham, cheese and salami.

Je voudrais deux sandwichs au jambon, un Coca et une orange pressée.

Jer voodray durr sondweech oh jombong, urn Coca ay ewn oronj pressay.
I would like two ham sandwiches, a Coca-Cola and an orange juice.

Une fourchette, s'il vous plaît.

Ewn foorshet, seelvooplay.
A fork, please.

Some things you might need to ask for

un couteau
urn kootoh
a knife

une carafe d'eau
ewn caraf doe
a jug of water

Ce n'est pas ce que j'ai commandé.

Sir nay pah sir ker jay commonday.
This is not what I ordered.

une cuiller
ewn kwee-air
a spoon

un verre
urn vair
a glass

une serviette
ewn sairvee-ett
a napkin

le sel et le poivre
ler sell ay ler pwarvr
salt and pepper

Où sont les toilettes?

Oo song lay twullett?
Where is the toilet?

Monsieur!

Moosyer!
Waiter!

L'addition, s'il vous plaît.

Ladeesseeong, seelvooplay.
The bill, please.

Est-ce que le service est compris?

Essker ler sairveess ay compree?
Is service included?

Going to a Restaurant

Restaurants usually display the menu in the window outside. Look out for restaurants with a sign saying *Relais Routiers*. In these you can get a good meal at a very reasonable price. A *brasserie* is a cheap restaurant which serves draught beer and simple meals.

Booking a table

Je voudrais réserver une table pour quatre à 20 heures.

Jer voodray rayzairvay ewn tarbl poor kattr ah vant urr.
I would like to book a table for four at 8 p.m.

Avez-vous une table pour quatre?

Avay-voozewn tarbl poor kattr?
Have you a table for four?

Avez-vous réservé?

Avay-voo rayzairvay?
Have you booked?

Avez-vous une table dans le jardin?

Avay-vooz ewn tarbl dong ler jardang?
Have you a table in the garden?

Etes-vous prêt à commander?

Ett-voo pret ah commonday?
Are you ready to order?

Comment préparez-vous ce plat?

Commong prayparay-voo sir plah?
How is this dish cooked?

Avez-vous quelque chose de très simple?

Avay-voo kellker showz der tray sampl?
Have you got anything very plain?

Drinks

Est-ce que je pourrais voir la carte des vins?

Essker jer pooray vwar lah cart day vang?
Could I see the wine list?

Je voudrais une carafe de vin ordinaire, et une bouteille d'eau minérale.

Jer voodray ewn caraf der vang ordeenair, ay ewn bootay doe meenairall.
I would like a carafe of house wine and a bottle of mineral water.

Nous sommes un peu pressés.

Noo somms urn per pressay.
We are in a bit of a hurry.

Qu'est-ce que vous me recommandez?

Kessker voo mer recommonday?
What do you recommend?

Qu'est-ce que vous avez comme jus de fruits?

Kessker vooz avay komm jew der frwee?
What soft drinks have you got?

Excusez-moi, j'ai renversé mon verre.

Exkewzay mwah, jay ronvairsay mong vair.
I'm sorry, I've spilt my drink.

Problems with the bill

Qu'est-ce que cela veut dire?

Kessker sirlah ver deer?
What does this mean?

The Menu

Café Menu

Café complet
Caffay complay
Continental breakfast

Pain grillé
Pang greeyay
Toast

Croissant
Cwassong
Crescent-shaped roll

Beurre et confiture
Burr ay konfeetyour
Butter and jam

Croque-Monsieur
Crock Moosyer
**Welsh Rarebit
with ham**

Omelette
Omlett
Omelette

Croque-Madame
Crock Madarm
**Welsh Rarebit with
ham and fried egg**

Salade mixte
Salad meext
Mixed salad

Sandwich
Sondweech
Sandwich

Quiche Lorraine
Keesh Lorrenn
Egg and bacon flan

Glaces
Glass
Ice cream

Les Consommations
Lay Consom-asseeon
Drinks

Pâtisserie
Pateessree
Pastries and cakes

Café
Caffay
Coffee (black)

Fromage
Fromarj
Cheese

Café au lait
Caffay oh lay
White coffee

Oeuf dur
Urf dyoor
Hard-boiled egg

Chocolat chaud
Shokolah show
Hot chocolate

Pommes frites
Pomm freet
Chips

Thé
Tay
Tea

Orange pressée
Oranj pressay
Fresh orange juice

Restaurant menu

Keep a look out for menus which advertise a special set meal, called a *Menu du Jour, Menu à Prix Fixe* or a *Menu Touristique*. They are cheaper than eating *A la Carte,* where you can choose anything on the menu you like.
Remember that there is usually a cover charge *(le couvert)* for each person.

La Carte

Assiette de crudités
Assee-ett der crewdeetay
Plate of raw vegetables

Les escargots
Lez escargo
Snails

Les cuisses de grenouilles
Lay cwees der grenoo-ee
Frogs legs

Les Entrées
Lez ontray
Main courses

Boeuf bourguignon
Berf boorgeenyon
Beef cooked in red wine

Selle d'agneau
Sell danyo
Saddle of lamb

Poulet à l'estragon
Poolay ah lestra-gone
Chicken in tarragon sauce

Médaillons de veau
Med-eye-ong der voe
Veal steaks

Rôti de porc
Roetee der porr
Roast pork

Canard aux cerises
Canarr oh sereez
Duck with cherries

Les Poissons
Lay pwusson
Fish

Moules
Mool
Mussels

Les crustacés
Lay kroostassay
Shell fish

Le homard
Ler ommar
Lobster

Les Légumes
Lay legyoom
Vegetables

Les Entremets
Lez ontrer-may
Puddings

Fromage
Le plateau de fromages
Ler plattoh der fromarj
Cheese board

Tarte aux pommes
Tart oh pomm
Apple tart

Crêpes
Crepp
Pancakes

Plat du jour
Plah dew joor
Today's special dish

T.V.A.
V.A.T.

Service non compris
Sairvees nong compree
Service not included

Entertainments 1

You should be able to find out what you can see from a local paper, the Tourist Office *(Syndicat d'Initiative)*, or the hotel receptionist. Smoking is forbidden in cinemas and theatres. You are expected to tip the usherette.

Qu'est-ce que vous pouvez me conseiller comme spectacle à voir ?

Kessker voo poovay mer consay-yay comm specktarckl ah vwar?
Can you recommend a show to see?

Le Cirque
Ler Seerk
Circus

Théâtre de Marionnettes
Tayartr der Marry-o-nett
Puppet Theatre

Un Dessin Animé
Urn Dessang Aneemay
Cartoon Film

Théâtre en Plein Air
Tayartr ong Plen Air
Open-Air Theatre

Une Fête Foraine
Ewn Fet Foren
Fairground

Une Pantomime
Ewn Porntomeem
A Pantomime

Son et Lumière
Song ay Lewmee-air
Sound and Light Show
(These tell the story of famous old buildings, in which they are held.)

Le Magicien
Ler Majeesee-an
Magician

Un Match de Football
Urn Match dur Football
Football Match

Qu'est-ce qu'on joue au cinéma ce soir?

Est-ce qu'il y a un film en anglais?

Kesskong joo oh seenaymah sir swar?
What is on at the cinema tonight?

Esskeel ya urn feelm on ong-glay?
Is there a film in English?

Quel est le prix des places?

Deux places à l'orchestre.

Kell ay ler pree day plass?
How much are the tickets?

Durr plass ah lorkesstr.
Two seats in the stalls.

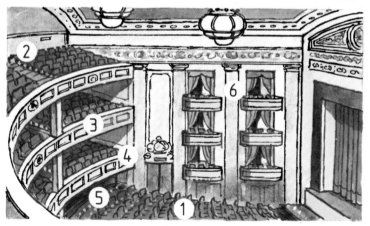

1 L'orchestre
Lorkesstr
The Stalls

2 La Galerie
Lah Galree
The Gallery

3 Le Deuxième Balcon
Ler Derzee-em Balcong
Upper Circle

4 La Corbeille
Lah Corbay
First Circle

5 Les Baignoires
Lay Baynwar
Dress Circle

6 Les Loges d'Avant-Scène
Lay Loj Davong Senn
Boxes

Entertainments 2

A quelle heure commence le spectacle ?

A 18 heures 30. Il se termine à 20 heures.

Ah kell urr commorss ler specktarckl ?
What time does the show begin ?

Ah deezweet urr tront. Eel sir tairmeen ah vant urr.
At six-thirty p.m. It finishes at eight o'clock.

Où est-ce que je peux acheter un programme, s'il vous plaît ?

L'ouvreuse en vend.

Oo essker jer per ashtay urn program, seelvooplay ?
Where can I buy a programme, please ?

Loovrerz ong von.
The usherette sells them.

Theatre signs

Cloakroom

Fire Exit

Toilets

No Smoking

INTERDIT AUX MOINS DE 18 ANS

INTERDIT AUX MOINS DE 13 ANS

These signs mean that children under the ages of 18 or 13 are not allowed to see the show.

This sign means that the show is a great success.

Sightseeing 1

The *Syndicat d'Initiative* or *Office de Tourisme* will also give you sightseeing information. You will usually have to pay an entrance fee to places of interest. Museums are often closed on Mondays or Tuesdays, and some places are closed in winter.

> Qu'est-ce qu'il y a d'intéressant à voir dans la ville?

Kesskeel ya dantairessong ah vwar dong lah veel?

What is there of interest to see in the town?

Places to go sightseeing

Le Château
Ler Shattoh
The Castle

Le Jardin Zoologique
Ler Jardang Zo-olojeek
The Zoo

Le Musée
Ler Mewzay
The Museum

L'Église
Leggleez
The Church

Le Vieux Quartier
Ler Vyer Kartee-yay
Old Part of Town

Parc National
Park Nasseeonal
Nature Reserve

Les Grottes
Lay Grott
Caves

> Est-ce qu'il y a un plan touristique de la ville?

Esskeel ya urn plong tooristeek der lah veel?

Is there a tourist map of the town?

> Est-ce que vous pouvez me dire quand le musée est ouvert?

Essker voo poovay mer deer cong ler mewzay ett oovair?

Can you tell me when the museum is open?

> Tous les jours sauf le mardi, de 9 heures à 18 heures.

Too lay joor sohf ler mardee, der nerf urr ah deezwet urr.

Every day except Tuesday, from 9 a.m. to 6 p.m.

> Quel est le prix de l'entrée?

Kell ay ler pree der lontray?

How much is the admission charge?

Sightseeing 2

Guided tours

Y a-t-il une visite guidée en anglais ?

Ee ateel ewn vizeet geeday ong ong-glay?
Is there a guided tour in English ?

Oui. La prochaine visite commence dans un quart d'heure.

Wee. Lah proshain vizeet commonss donz urn kar durr.
Yes. The next tour starts in a quarter of an hour.

La visite prend combien de temps ?

Lah vizeet prong combeeyen der tong?
How long does the tour last ?

Peut-on monter en haut de la tour?

Pert ong montay on oh der lah toor?
Can one go up the tower ?

At the zoo

Le Vivarium
Ler Veevaree-oom
Reptile House

La Volière
Lah Volee-air
The Aviary

Les Singes
Lay Sanj
Monkey House

Le Goûter des Chimpanzés
Ler Gootay day Shimpanza
Chimpanzees Tea-Party

La Fosse aux Ours
Lah Foss oh Oors
Bear Pit

Promenade à dos d'âne
Promenard ah doe dan
Donkey rides

Promenade à chameau
Promernard ah shamoh
Camel rides

Signs

Do not Feed
the Animals

Dangerous
Animals

Wild Animals

Entrance

Exit

Do not Touch

Cameras Prohibited

Tea-Room

Private Property

Beware of
the Dog

No Entrance

Closed for
the Holidays

Open

Closed

Keep off
the Grass

Making Friends

Bongjoor. Commong tappell tew?
Hello. What is your name?

Jer mappell Marree. Ay twa?
My name is Mary. And yours?

Oo pass tew lay vackonss?
Where are you staying?

Jabeet lah bah.
I live over there.

Kell arj ah tew?   Jay dooz ong.
How old are you?   I'm 12.

Vwussee mong frair Jong. Ah tew frair ay sir?
This is my brother John. Have you any brothers and sisters?

We. Jay ewn sir aynay, ay vwussee mong frair jewmoh.
Yes. I have an elder sister, and this is my twin brother.

100

Pouvez-vous déjeuner avec nous?

Poovay voo dayjernay aveck noo?
Can you have lunch with us?

Il faut que je demande à nos parents.

Eel foe ker jer demond ah no parong.
I must ask my parents.

On va jouer.

Ong vah jooay
Let's go and play!

Dépêchez-vous!

J'arrive!

Attends-moi!

Daypeshay voo! Jarreev! Attong-mwa!
Hurry up! I'm coming! Wait for me!

J'aime...

Jaim...
I like..

Jeu d'échecs
Jer daysheck
Chess

La Peinture
Lah Pantewr
Painting

La Menuiserie
Lah Menweezeree
Woodwork

La Philatélie
Lah Feelataylee
Stamp Collectin

Cards

Les Carreaux
Lay Carroh
Diamonds

Les Cœurs
Lay Curr
Hearts

Les Trèfles
Lay Treffl
Clubs

Les Piques
Lay Peek
Spades

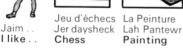

Le Roi
Ler Rwah
King

La Reine
Lah Renn
Queen

Le Valet
Ler Vallay
Jack

L'As
Lass
Ace

Le Joker
Ler Jokair
Joker

Playing Games

La balançoire
Lah Balongswar
Swing

Lance-moi la balle!

Attrape!

Lahnce mwa lah barl!
Throw me the ball!

Attrapp!
Catch!

Cache-Cache
Cash-Cash
Hide and Seek

Saute-Mouton
Sote-Mootong
Leap Frog

A quoi jouez-vous?

Ça s'appelle la Pétanque.

Sa sappell lah Pettongk.
It's called Pétanque.

Ah kwa jooay-voo?
What are you playing?

103

Sports

There is a lot of good fishing in France, especially for trout, pike and salmon. For river and lake fishing, you must join an anglers' association *(une association de pêche et de pisciculture)*. To do this, ask at a fishing tackle shop.

Going fishing

Où est-ce que je peux louer une canne à pêche?

Oo essker jer per looay ewn cann ah pesh?
Where can I hire a fishing-rod?

Ça fait combien pour la journée?

Sah fay combeeyen poor lah jornay?
How much does it cost for the day?

Faut-il avoir un permis?

Foe-teel avwar urn pairmee?
Must one have a permit?

Avez-vous des appâts, s'il vous plaît?

Avay-voo dez appah, seelvooplay?
Have you any bait, please?

Est-ce un bon endroit pour pêcher?

Ess urn bong ondrwa poor peshay?
Is this a good place to fish?

Riding

Peut-on monter à cheval près d'ici?

Pert-ong montay ah sherval pray dee-see?
Can one go riding near here?

Nous voudrions prendre des cours d'équitation.

Noo voodreeong prondr day coor deckee tasseeong.
We would like some riding lessons.

Skiing

Les Chaussures de Ski	Les Skis	Les Bâtons de Ski	Les Gants de Ski	Un Abonnement
Lay Showsyoor der Skee	Lay Skee	Lay Battong der Skee	Lay Gong der Skee	Urn Abonmong
Ski Boots	**Skis**	**Ski Sticks**	**Ski Gloves**	**Ski Pass**

Où se trouve l'école de ski?

Oo sir troov leckoll dur skee?
Where is the ski school?

The ski runs

The ski runs, or *Pistes*, are marked with coloured arrows.

Nursery slopes - very easy.

Beginners - easy.

For quite experienced skiers - quite difficult.

For professional skiers - very difficult.

Je suis débutant.

J'ai déjà skié une fois.

Je suis assez fort.

Jer swee debewtong.
I am a beginner.

Jay dayja skeeay ewn fwah.
I have skied once before.

Jer swee assay for.
I am quite experienced.

Je ne peux pas me lever. Pouvez-vous m'aider?

Jer ner per pah mer levay. Poovay-voo mayday?
I cannot get up. Can you help me?

Nous sommes perdus. Où est le téléski?

Noo somm pairdew. Oo ay ler taylayskee?
We are lost. Where is the ski-lift?

At the Seaside 1

Où est la plage la plus proche?

Oo ay lah plarj lah plew prosh?
Where is the nearest beach?

Y a-t-il une piscine?

Ee ateel ewn pesseen?
Is there a swimming pool?

Je voudrais louer deux matelas, une chaise longue . . .

Jer voodray looay durr materlah, ewn shairz longg . . .
I would like to hire two mattresses, a deck chair . . .

. . . et un parasol.

. . . ay urn parasol.
. . . and a parasol.

Où est-ce que je peux me changer?

A côté du bassin.

Oo essker jer per mer shongjay?
Where are the changing rooms?
Ah coatay dew bassang.
Next to the paddling pool.

Beach things

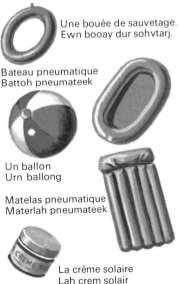

Une bouée de sauvetage.
Ewn booay dur sohvtarj.

Bateau pneumatique
Battoh pneumateek

Un ballon
Urn ballong

Matelas pneumatique
Materlah pneumateek

La crème solaire
Lah crem solair

106

Bonjour. On va se baigner?

Bongjoor. Ong vah sir baynyay?
Hello. Let's go for a swim.

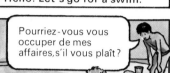

Pourriez-vous vous occuper de mes affaires, s'il vous plaît?

Pooree-ay voo vooz ockewpay der mez affair, seelvooplay?
Please could you look after my things for me?

Attention! Voilà une grosse vague!

Attongseeong! Vwullah ewn gross varg!
Watch out! There's a big wave coming!

Y a-t-il une douche?

Ee ateel ewn doosh?
Is there a shower?

Passe-moi la serviette.

Pass mwah lah sairveeyet.
Pass me the towel.

Le Ski Nautique
Ler Skee Nohteek
Water Skiing

Les Cours de Natation
Lay Coor dur Natasseeong
Swimming Lessons

Pédalos
Pedalow
Pedaloes

Voiliers
Vwullee-ay
Sailing Boats

At the Seaside 2

On construit un château de sable?

As-tu un seau et une pelle?

Ong constrwee urn shattoh dur sarbl?
Shall we build a sand castle?

Ah-tew urn soe ay ewn pell?
Have you got a bucket and spade?

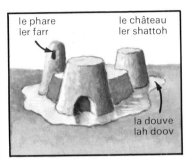

le phare
ler farr

le château
ler shattoh

la douve
lah doov

Que signifie le drapeau rouge?

Ker seenyeefee ler drapoh rooj?
What does the red flag mean?

Il est dangereux de se baigner. La mer est trop agitée.

DÉFENSE DE SE BAIGNER

Eel ay dongjay-rer der sir baynyay. Lah mair ay troh ajeetay.
It is dangerous to swim. The sea is too rough.

No Bathing

J'ai chaud.

Jay show.
I'm hot.

On va acheter une glace?

GLACES

Ong vah ashtay ewn glass?
Let's go and buy an ice cream.

108

Buying an ice cream

Excusez-moi. Avez-vous des glaces?
Exkewsay mwah. Avay voo day glass?
Excuse me. Do you have any ice creams?

Oui. Quel parfum voulez-vous?
We. Kel parfang voolay voo?
Yes. What flavour would you like?

Vanille
Vanee
Vanilla

Fraise
Frairz
Strawberry

Framboise
Frombwarz
Raspberry

Praliné
Praleenay
Nutty

Pistache
Peestash
Pistachio

Chocolat
Shok-o-lah
Chocolate

Je voudrais une glace à la vanille.
Jer voodray ewn glass ah lah vanee.
I would like a vanilla ice.

Une simple ou une double?
Ewn sampl oo ewn doobl?
A single or a double cornet?

Une double et un esquimau à la fraise.
Ewn doobl ay urn eskimo ah lah frairz.
A double and a strawberry lolly.

Ça fait combien?
Sa fay combeeyen?
How much is that?

Trois francs.
Trwa frong.
Three francs.

Merci.
Mairsee.
Thank you.

Accidents and Emergencies

The numbers for fire, police and ambulance services are given on the central disc of the telephone (see page 80). Road accidents should be reported to the police station *(Gendarmerie)* immediately. If you are in serious trouble, contact a British Consulate.

Au secours!

Oh sircoor!
Help!

Venez vite!

Vernay vite!
Come quickly!

Au feu!

Oh furr!
Fire!

Appelez une ambulance, s'il vous plaît.

Applay ewn ombewlonss, seelvooplay.
Please call for an ambulance.

Missing persons

Mon ami est absent depuis hier soir.

Mong amee ett absong derpwee ee-air swar.
My friend has been missing since last night.

Quand l'avez-vous vu pour la dernière fois?

Kong lavay voo vew poor lah dairneeair fwa?
When did you last see him?

Il est sorti à 18 heures pour acheter un journal.

Eel ay sortee ah deezweet urr poor ashtay urn joornal.
He went out at 6.00 p.m. to buy a newspaper.

Il portait une écharpe et un chapeau rouges.

Eel portay ewn esharp ay urn shappoh rooj.
He was wearing a red scarf and hat.

Lost or stolen

> J'ai perdu mon passeport.

Jay pairdew mong passporr.
I have lost my passport.

> On m'a volé mon porte feuille.

Ong mah volay mong port-foy.
My wallet has been stolen.

> On a cambriolé ma chambre.

Ong ah combree-olay mah shormbr.
My room has been burgled.

> Où pouvons-nous vous contacter?

Oo poovong noo voo contacktay?
Where can we contact you?

Other things

mes chèques de voyage
may sheck dur vweye-arj
my traveller's cheques

mon appareil photographique
mong apparay fotografeek
my camera

ma valise
mah valeez
my suitcase

mes clefs
may clay
my keys

mon sac
mong sack
my bag

ma montre
mah montr
my watch

> Ça s'est passé entre 10 heures et midi.

Sa say passay ontr deess urr ay meedee.
It happened between 10.00 a.m. and midday.

> Voici mon nom et mon adresse.

Vwussee mong nom ay mong address.
Here is my name and address.

111

Using the Telephone

You will find public telephones in post offices and most cafés. Some are operated by coins, others by special tokens, called *jetons,* which you can buy in the post office or café. Long distance and international calls have to be connected by the operator.

On coin-operated phones, you usually have to insert the coin before dialling. The dialling tone is a high-pitched buzz. After you have dialled, you will hear a series of short pips while the line is connecting. Then you will hear the ringing tone —a long buzz followed by a short pause.

On *jeton*-operated phones, do not put the token in until someone answers.

The telephone dial

This is what the names in the centre of the dial mean.

Renseignements
Ronsaynyemong
Enquiries

Réclamations
Rayclamasseeong
Out of Order

Télégraphe
Taylay graf
Telegrams

Police-Secours
Poleess-Sekoor
Police

Pompiers
Pompeeyay
Fire Brigade

Making a phone call

Est-ce que je peux me servir du téléphone, s'il vous plaît ?

Essker jer per mer sairveer dew taylayfone, seelvooplay ?
Please may I use the telephone?

Puis-je avoir trois jetons, s'il vous plaît ?

Pwee javwar twah jurtong, seelvooplay ?
Please may I have three telephone tokens?

Je voudrais appeler Londres en P.C.V. Le numéro est 800 6009 à Londres.

Jer voodray zapplay Londr ong Pay Say Vay. Ler newmairo ay weet song, swussont, zairo, nerf ah Londr.
I want to call London and reverse the charges. The number is London 800 6009.

Quel est votre numéro ?
Ne quittez pas.

Kell ay vottr newmairo ? Ner keetay pah.
What is your number ? Hold the line.

Vous vous êtes trompé de numéro.

Voo vooz ett trompay der newmairo.
You have the wrong number.

Est-ce que je pourrais parler à M. Dupont, s'il vous plaît ?

Essker jer per parlay ah Moosyer Dewpong, seelvooplay?
Please may I speak to Mr Dupont ?

Le numéro est occupé.

Ler newmairo ett ockewpay.
The number is engaged.

Il n'est pas ici en ce moment.

C'est de la part de qui ?

Eel nay paz ee-see ong sir momong.
He is not here at the moment.

Say dur lah par dur kee ?
Who is speaking ?

Pourriez-vous lui dire que Mme Brown a téléphoné, et lui demander de m'appeler à ce numéro.

Pooree-ay voo lwee deer ker Madamm Brown a taylayfonay, ay lwee demongday der mapplay ah sir newmairo.
Could you tell him that Mrs Brown telephoned, and ask him to ring me at this number

Feeling Ill

The *pharmacie* will be able to give you advice and medicine for most minor ailments. If you see a doctor, you will have to pay him on the spot. Residents of E.E.C. countries can get most of their money refunded, when they get home, if they have to pay for hospital treatment.

J'ai mal à la tête.
Jay mal ah lah tet.
I have a headache.

J'ai mal au ventre.
Jay mal oh vorntr.
I have a stomach pain.

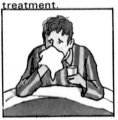

Je suis enrhumé.
Jer sweez onrewmay.
I have a cold.

Je tousse énormément.
Jer tooss aynormaymong.
I am coughing a lot.

J'ai de la fièvre.
Jay dur lah fee-airvr.
I have a temperature.

J'ai mal au cœur.
Jay mal oh curr.
I feel sick.

Je me suis coupé.
Jer mer swee coopay
I have cut myself.

Je me suis brûlé.
Jer mer swee brewlay.
I have burnt myself.

J'ai attrapé un coup de soleil.
Jay attrapay urn coo der solay.
I am sunburnt.

Je me suis fait piquer par . . .
Jer mer swee fay peekay par . . .
I have been stung (or bitten) by . . .

. . . une méduse.
. . . ewn medewz.
. . . a jellyfish.

. . . un oursin.
. . . urn oorsang.
. . . a sea-urchin.

. . . un serpent.
. . . urn sairpong.
. . . a snake.

. . une guêpe.
. . . ewn gepp.
. . . a wasp.

114

J'ai quelque chose
dans l'œil.
Jay kellker showz
dong loy.
**I have something in
my eye.**

J'ai une éruption.
Jay ewn eroopsseeong.
I have a rash.

Ça me gratte.
Sa mer gratt.
It itches.

J'ai mal aux dents.
Jay mal oh dong.
I have toothache.

J'ai été attaqué par un
chien.
Jay ettay attackay par
urn shee-en.
**I have been attacked
by a dog.**

Je me suis cassé la
jambe.
Jer mer swee cassay
lah jomb.
I have broken my leg.

Going to the doctor

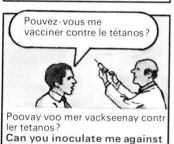

Il me faut voir un
médecin.

Eel mer foe vwar urn medsang.
I need to see a doctor.

Quand est-il libre ?

Kont est eel leebr ?
When is he free ?

Pouvez-vous me
vacciner contre le tétanos ?

Poovay voo mer vackseenay contr
ler tetanos ?
**Can you inoculate me against
tetanus ?**

Pouvez-vous me donner
une ordonnance ?

Poovay-voo mer donnay ewn
ordononss ?
Can you give me a prescription?

Parts of the Body

la tête
lah tett
head

les cheveux
lay shervur
hair

les yeux
lez yer
eyes

le nez
ler nay
nose

les oreilles
lez orray
ears

la bouche
lah boosh
mouth

le cou
ler coo
neck

le menton
ler montong
chin

l'épaule
leppoal
shoulder

le visage
ler veezarj
face

le coude
ler cood
elbow

la poitrine
lah pwutreen
chest

le dos
ler doe
back

la main
lah mang
hand

le bras
ler brah
arm

le poignet
ler pweye-nyay
wrist

la hanche
lah aunsh
hip

l'estomac
lestoh-mah
stomach

le doigt
ler dwah
finger

la jambe
la jormb
leg

le genou
ler jernoo
knee

la cheville
lah sheveey
ankle

le doigt de pied
ler dwah der pee-ay
toe

le pied
ler pee-ay
foot

Il est grand.
Eel ay grong.
He is tall.

Il est jeune.
Eel ay jern.
He is young.

Il est petit.
Eel ay pertee.
He is short.

Elle est grosse.
Ell ay gross.
She is fat.

Elle est mince.
Ell ay manse.
She is thin.

Elle est vieille.
Ell ay veeay.
She is old.

116

Colours
Les Couleurs (Lay Coolurr)

noir
nwar
black

blanc
blong
white

gris
gree
grey

beige
bairj
beige

brun
bruh
brown

jaune
joan
yellow

orange
oronj
orange

rouge
rooj
red

rose
roz
pink

violet
vee-olay
violet

bleu
bler
blue

vert
vair
green

or
or
gold

argent
arjong
silver

foncé
fonsay
dark

clair
clair
light

117

Months, Seasons and Days

Janvier
Jonveeyay
January

Février
Fevreeyay
February

Mars
Marss
March

Avril
Avreel
April

Mai
May
May

Juin
Jwang
June

Juillet
Jweeyay
July

Août
Oot
August

Septembre
Septombr
September

Octobre
Ocktobr
October

Novembre
Novombr
November

Décembre
Dayssombr
December

La Semaine (Lah Sirmen)

7 Lundi
Lurndee
Monday

8 Mardi
Mardee
Tuesday

9 Mercredi
Mairkrerdee
Wednesday

Déjeuner avec Jean

10 Jeudi
Jerdee
Thursday

11 Vendredi
Vondrerdee
Friday

12 Samedi
Samdee
Saturday

Dentiste

13 Dimanche
Deemonsh
Sunday

Les Saisons (Lay Sezong)

Le Printemps
Ler Prantong
The Spring

L'été
Lettay
The Summer

L'automne
Lohtonn
The Autumn

L'hiver
Leevair
The Winter

The Weather

Le Temps
(Ler Tong)

Il pleut.
Eel pler.
It's raining.

Il va pleuvoir.
Eel vah plervwar.
It's going to rain.

La grêle
Lah grell
Hail

Il y a du vent.
Eel ya dew vong.
It's windy.

Il neige.
Eel nairj.
It's snowing.

Il y a des nuages.
Eel ya day newarj.
It's cloudy.

Le tonnerre
Ler tonnair
Thunder

Un éclair
Urn ecklair
A flash of lightning.

Quel orage!
Kell orarj
What a storm!

Il fait beau.
Eel fay boe.
It's a nice day.

Il fait chaud.
Eel fay show.
It is hot.

Il fait froid.
Eel fay frwah.
It is cold.

Il est dix heures et demie.
Eel ay deess urr ay dermee.
It is half past ten.

Il est minuit.
Eel ay meenwee.
It is midnight.

le matin
ler matang
the morning

l'après-midi
lappray meedee
the afternoon

le soir
ler swar
the evening

la nuit
lah nwee
the night

Time phrases

hier ee-air **yesterday**	cette année set annay **this year**	de bonne heure der bonn urr **early**	dans cinq minutes dong sank minewt **in five minutes**
aujourd'hui ohjoordwee **today**	le mois dernier ler mwah dairnee-ay **last month**	plus tôt plew toe **earlier**	dans un quart d'heure donz karr durr
demain dermang **tomorrow**	la semaine prochaine	bientôt bee-entoe **soon**	**in a quarter of an hour**
avant-hier avont-ee-air **the day before yesterday**	ah simen proshain **next week**	plus tard plew tar **later**	dans une demie- heure donz ewn dermee urr **in half an hour**
le lendemain ler londermang **the following day**	maintenant manthong **now**	jamais jamay **never**	dans une heure donz ewn urr **in an hour**

123

Basic Grammar

Nouns

All French nouns are either masculine or feminine. When you learn a noun, you must learn this as well. The word for "the" is *le* before masculine(m) nouns and *la* before feminine(f) nouns,

e.g. *le chien* (the dog)
la maison (the house).

If *le* or *la* comes before a noun beginning with a,e,i,o,u or h (with some exceptions), it becomes *l'*, e.g. *l'arbre* (the tree).

If the noun is plural (p), the word for "the" is *les*,
e.g. *les chiens* (the dogs)
les maisons (the houses)
les arbres (the trees).
In the plural, most French nouns have "s" on the end.

The French for "a" or "an" is *un* before masculine nouns and *une* before feminine nouns.
e.g. *un chien* (a dog)
une maison (a house).

This, that

The French use the same word for "this" and "that". It is *ce* before masculine nouns and *cette* before feminine nouns. If *ce* comes before a noun beginning with a,e,i,o or u, it becomes *cet*. The word for "these" or "those" is *ces*.

e.g. *ce chien*   (this dog)
cette maison (this house)
cet arbre   (this tree)
ces chiens   (these dogs)
ces maisons   (these houses)
ces arbres   (these trees)

Pronouns

The French word for "it" or "they" depends on whether the noun it replaces is masculine or feminine,
e.g. *le chien mange* (the dog eats)
il mange   (it eats)

I	je
you	tu
he, it (m)	il
she, it (f)	elle
we	nous
you (p)	vous
they (m)	ils
they (f)	elles

Possessive adjectives

The word you use for "my", "your", "his" etc. depends on whether the word that follows it is masculine, feminine or plural,

e.g. *mon chien* (m) (my dog)
sa maison (f)   (his or her house)
tes frères (p) (your brothers)

	(m)	(f)	(p)
my	mon	ma	mes
your	ton	ta	tes
his, hers, its	son	sa	ses
our	notre	notre	nos
your (p)	votre	votre	vos
their	leur	leur	leurs

Useful verbs

avoir	to have
j'ai	I have
tu as	you have
il a	he/it has
elle a	she/it has
nous avons	we have
vous avez	you have (p)
ils ont	they have (m)
elles ont	they have (f)

être	to be
je suis	I am
tu es	you are
il est	he/it is
elle est	she/it is
nous sommes	we are
vous êtes	you are (p)
ils sont	they are (m)
elles sont	they are (f)

parler	to speak
je parle	I speak
tu parles	you speak
il parle	he/it speaks
elle parle	she/it speaks
nous parlons	we speak
vous parlez	you speak (p)
ils parlent	they speak (m)
elles parlent	they speak (f)

venir	to come
je viens	I come
tu viens	you come
il vient	he/it comes
elle vient	she/it comes
nous venons	we come
vous venez	you come (p)
ils viennent	they come (m)
elles viennent	they come (f)

aller	to go
je vais	I go
tu vas	you go
il va	he/it goes
elle va	she/it goes
nous allons	we go
vous allez	you go (p)
ils vont	they go (m)
elles vont	they go (f)

vouloir	to want
je veux	I want
tu veux	you want
il veut	he/it wants
elle veut	she/it wants
nous voulons	we want
vous voulez	you want (p)
ils veulent	they want (m)
elles veulent	they want (f)

Negatives

To make a verb negative, add *ne* before the verb and *pas* after it. If *ne* comes before a vowel, it becomes *n'*,

e.g. je parle français	I speak French
je ne parle pas français	I do not speak French
j'ai	I have
je n'ai pas	I have not

Questions.....

There are two ways you can ask a question in French. You can either put the verb before the pronoun, or you can use the phrase *est-ce que* at the beginning of the question,

e.g. *vous voulez*	you want
voulez-vous?	do you want?
est-ce que vous voulez?	do you want?

Index

This index lists some words individually and some under group names, such as food. Where you will find the French for the indexed word, the page number is printed in italics, like this: *6*.

Index of French words

This index lists some of the French words you might see on signs and notices. Look up the page reference to find out what they mean.

PRINTED IN BELGIUM BY

proost
INTERNATIONAL BOOK PRODUCTION